The CHRISTIAN *philosophy of* EDUCATION *explained*

The CHRISTIAN *philosophy of* EDUCATION *explained*

Stephen C. Perks

Whitby

AVANT BOOKS

England

1992

Published in Great Britain by
AVANT BOOKS
P. O. Box 1, Whitby, North Yorkshire,
YO21 1HP, England

ISBN 0-9518899-0-7

British Library Cataloguing-in-Publication Data.
A catalogue record for this book is available from the British Library.

Printed and bound in Great Britain by
Biddles Ltd, Guildford, Surrey

PREFACE

The deterioration of academic standards and discipline in state schools in Britain in the last twenty-five years has finally forced the issue of education upon the consciences of many Christians who would not otherwise have considered it. There is both good and bad in this. The crisis in state education has led some to reconsider the whole issue of education and the place of Christian children in a state system which promotes secular humanism and multi-culturalism as a virtue, and discourages the traditional Christian world-view and its code of morality. This is surely good. Yet the fact that it has taken such a crisis to awaken Christian parents to their responsibilities *as* Christians in this area is indicative of a serious failure in the church's understanding of its calling in this world. It is a sad indictment upon the church's ministry, in particular, that this issue needed to be *forced* upon the consciences of Christians at all, but especially by a crisis in the practice of an alien religion, namely secular humanism, with which the church has compromised itself.

In this situation there are many voices offering many different solutions to the problem. Some Christian pressure groups and parliamentary lobbying groups have tried to introduce measures into the law aimed at Christianising the state education system, others at securing state funding for so-called independent Christian schools. A few advocate the withdrawal of all education, Christian or otherwise, from the orbit of state authority and funding. In this situation it is important that all the relevant issues should be considered carefully in the light of biblical teaching. Only when this has been done are we in a position to make an intelligent decision about the correct Christian response. The aim of this book is to explain the Christian philosophy of education and thereby help those who read it to make that Christian response.

Two of the chapters in this book have been published previously: Chapter One was originally published in *Calvinism Today*, vol. I, no. 1 (January 1991) as "The Epistemological Basis of the Sola Scriptura Conception of Theology," and Chapter Three was published by The Foundation for Christian Reconstruction as *Position Paper 1* in April 1991. Chapter Two was originally given as a workshop at the Eleventh Annual Conference for Christian Reconstruction in Seattle, Washington, USA, in April 1991. Appendix A, "Scripture and the Covenants," was originally published in a slightly modified form by The Foundation for Christian Reconstruction in December 1988, and a shorter version of Appendix B was published in the *Chalcedon Report* (no. 305) in December 1990. In spite of this, however, the book is not merely a collection of essays and was originally conceived as a whole.

TABLE OF CONTENTS

INTRODUCTION

The test of the church's relevance to society in any age is in the radically biblical stance it takes towards the vital issues of the era and, by its biblical approach to those issues, its positive transforming effect on society. This was the case with the Reformation. It is no less the case today. The strength of the Reformation church was that it recognised and dealt with the vital issues of the day in terms of the requirements of biblical faith. The weakness of the church today, including most Reformed and evangelical churches, is in the fact that it does not recognise and deal adequately with the issues facing it in the twentieth century.

Education is one of those issues. Indeed, education is likely to be the single most important and strategic issue facing the Christian in the years ahead as he struggles to engage in the Christian reconstruction of the nation. Without the development of a self-consciously Christian educational movement there will be no reconstruction of our nation in terms of the Christian faith. Education is the high ground in the Christian's battle with the forces of humanism and atheism, which control so much of our lives and which, were they able, would deny to the Christian his God-given responsibility to provide an education for his children which is in conformity with the demands of the Christian religion.

It is vitally important, therefore, if we are to be salt and light to our generation, that we address this crucial issue and develop an understanding of the Christian principles relevant to the philosophy and practice of education. It is particularly important that the *church* should take a positive stance over this issue, that it should make a determined and sustained effort to reverse those attitudes within the church which are apathetic and hostile to the provision of a specifically Christian philosophy and practice of education, and that it should start promoting and facilitating as best it can a programme of re-education regarding the responsibilities of Christian parents in this area. Furthermore, the church must consider whether the present situation, in which there is such a dearth of provision for Christian education, constitutes a mission field that the church should explore.

The purpose of this book is to elucidate some of the most important aspects of the Christian philosophy of education. It should be said at the outset, however, that the philosophy of education set forth here is based self-consciously on a distinctive understanding of the Christian faith and argued in terms of that understanding at all points, namely, that the source for our understanding of what Christianity is, and hence the sole criterion for establishing its content, is the infallible word of God revealed in the scriptures of the Old and New Testaments. In other words the philosophy of education set forth in this book will be based on the *sola scriptura* conception of the Christian religion. These Scriptures will be understood as the supreme and governing authority for our understanding of all things and hence for our understanding of the nature, purpose and method of a truly Christian education.

It will be necessary first of all, therefore, to establish the epistemological validity of the theological presuppositions upon which this understanding of the Christian faith rests. These epistemological considerations are dealt with in Chapter One. Chapter Two deals with the role that our definition of man plays in the philosophy and process of education. Here the current humanist concept of the primacy—and hence the idolising—of the peer group is considered, in contrast to the Christian view of the image of God in man, which is the primary factor in the Christian philosophy of education. Chapter Three deals with education as an aspect of the covenant. Chapter Four looks at the relevance of man's creation mandate for the Christian philosophy of education. Since education is a central aspect of the Christian parent's covenantal responsibilities, and since this covenant is a covenant of dominion in Jesus Christ, a truly Christian education must be an education for dominion. In Chapter Five Adam's naming of the animals is considered as a case study in godly learning. The significance of education in the preservation of our civilisation and the transmission of our culture to future generations is considered in Chapter Six, and the final chapter deals with the role that the local church as an institution should play in the provision of educational services under normal and abnormal circumstances. The issues dealt with in the two appendices, while not directly related to education, are included here since they help to shed light on the theological perspective which forms the basis for the philosophy of education set forth in this book.

1

THE EPISTEMOLOGICAL BASIS OF THE CHRISTIAN FAITH

The Scriptures are God's revelation both of Himself to man, and of His will for man. They reveal therefore not merely the truth, "what man is to believe concerning God," but also the command word of God, "what duty God requires of man" (Westminster Shorter Catechism Q. 3, *A*.). The task of theology, therefore, is twofold: first, the theologian aims to understand and communicate effectively the truth of God's word, and secondly, to apply the command word of God to the contemporary situation, thereby providing an intelligible basis for the practical outworking of the Christian faith.

This definition of the theological task makes certain assumptions about the relation between Scripture and theology, namely, that the Scriptures are the essential and fundamental basis for our understanding of God and of His works of creation and providence—in other words for our understanding of all things—and thus that the Bible speaks with final authority on all matters with which it deals. If we abandon this conception of the theological task we cut the essential tie between Scripture and theology.

This has been borne out by developments in modern Protestant theology, which has increasingly rejected the *sola scriptura* conception of theology in favour of a more Deist or rationalistic approach. No main-stream Protestant denomination or group within those denominations has been unaffected by this modern trend. The result has been that the Scriptures, as the source of ultimate truth, and even more so as the command word of God, have slipped into the background, and in the case of the latter have become almost totally neglected—in many quarters even as a basis for the teaching of ethics and personal morality. The essential tie between Scripture and theology has gone, and it has gone because the epistemological basis upon which it was predicated has been abandoned.

The purpose of this chapter is to examine the epistemological basis of the *sola scriptura* conception of the Christian faith in contrast to that of the non-believer's world-view,[1] and then to provide a brief application of the Christian theory of knowledge to the philosophy of education. The necessity and importance of dealing with this subject today is occasioned by the fact that epistemology is the overriding preoccupation of modern philosophy, and hence it is only on the basis of a proper understanding of the subject that we are able to mount an apologetics for the Christian faith which is both rationally consistent and at the same time faithful to Scripture.

The ultimate locus of rationality

The Austrian economist and philosopher Ludwig von Mises said that facts do not speak for themselves, they are spoken about by a theory. This is a typically post-Kantian statement, and as thus cited it means that the facts of reality have no

---

1. For much of what I have to say here on epistemology, and for my understanding of this subject generally, I am indebted to the writings of Cornelius Van Til. However, since most of his books do not have an index—and even where there is an index it is usually not exhaustive—I have been unable to give specific references to his writings for some of the ideas I have expressed, and therefore this general acknowledgement must suffice. For those who wish to pursue this subject in greater detail the following three books by Cornelius Van Til are excellent starting points: *A Survey of Christian Epistemology*, *The Defense of the Faith* and *A Christian Theory of Knowledge*, all published by Presbyterian and Reformed Publishing Company.

meaning or purpose until the creative mind of man orders those facts logically and thereby gives them meaning and purpose. In this perspective the ultimate locus of rationality and intelligibility is man himself. Man is the measure of all things beyond whom there is no higher authority. For the Christian, however, it is God's creative act which gives all the facts of reality their purpose and meaning. His word is the original creative word which brings into existence and orders all the facts of reality. Man is able to understand the world in which he lives because he too is a part of that rationally ordered creation, created in God's image "in knowledge, righteousness, and holiness, with dominion over the creatures."

What the non-believer asserts about the facts of reality, therefore, is based upon a particular theory of human knowledge which assumes that the mind of man has the original creative power to define and order the raw data of reality which surround him without reference to any outside authority or interpretive principle.[2] In other words it is based on certain presuppositions about the nature of the world in which he lives, viz. that the world exists and can be understood independently of the God of Scripture.

Likewise, what the Christian asserts about the facts of reality is based on a particular presupposition about the nature of reality, namely, that it is the creation *ex nihilo* of the God of

---

2. Writing on the secularisation of science Herman Dooyeweerd states: "The new ideal of science secularized the biblical motive of creation. Creative power was attributed to theoretical thought, to which was given the task of methodically demolishing the structures of reality as they are given in the divine order of creation, in order to create them again theoretically according to its own image.

"The proud statement of Descartes, repeated by Kant, 'Give us material and we shall construct a world for you,' and the statement of Thomas Hobbes, that theoretical thought can create just like God himself, are both inspired by the same humanistic motive, the motive of the creative freedom of man concentrated in scientific thought." (*The Secularization of Science* [Memphis, TN: Christian Studies Centre, 1954], p. 19.)

Scripture. Thus the Christian knows all things by faith (Heb. 11:3), that is to say he begins his thinking with an act of faith in the God of the Scriptures and thereby posits the veracity and sufficiency of divine revelation as the very foundation of his understanding of all things. In so doing he insists that the only valid interpretation of the facts of reality is that given them by their Creator and that this authoritative interpretation of reality has been set down by God Himself in the Scriptures of the Old and New Testaments. Thus the Christian asserts that the only valid epistemology or theory of human knowledge is that which is based on God's revealed word.

Hence, although we must reject outright the framework which gave rise to this dictum—viz. that facts do not speak for themselves but are spoken about by a theory—we must, however, at the same time recognise that there is also an important truth in it. Indeed, this truth is for man the fundamental basis of epistemology. But for the humanist it is the autonomous mind of man which makes sense of the facts of reality, which speaks the definitive word of truth about the realm of phenomena, whereas for the Christian it is God who speaks the word of truth about reality.[3]

For the Christian, therefore, the ultimate locus of rationality and intelligibility is the God of Scripture and thus man, if he is to know anything truly, must, as God's creature, created in His image, "think God's thoughts after Him," to use the words of Cornelius Van Til.

Moreover, the non-believer also, according to the Christian theory of knowledge, is only able to arrive at true knowledge to the same extent, though he is unaware that this is the case. To the extent that he denies this and refuses to think God's thoughts after Him his knowledge is false, since it is

---

3. The difference between these two approaches can perhaps be summed up by saying that this truth is for the Christian the *proximate* starting point in the act of knowing, whereas for the humanist it is the *ultimate* starting point.

based on a theory which does not accord with the Creator's definitive and authoritative interpretation of the facts of reality. The classic example of this is, of course, Eve's assessment of the facts of reality in the Garden of Eden. Having assumed that she had the ability to arrive at ultimate truth concerning the nature of reality without reference to the authoritative word of God she made a false assessment of the facts concerning the tree of the knowledge of good and evil. It is this process of autonomous reasoning, i.e. the rejection of God's definitive word as the foundation of all knowledge, which led to the fall and which constitutes the essence of original sin.

Some problems with the humanist view of rationality

The non-believer, as we have seen, starts his thinking with the premise that the world exists and can be understood independently of the God who created it and upholds it continually by the word of His power. He thereby posits an epistemology which he claims is *neutral* or *objective*, i.e. based on the facts of reality rather than the facts being interpreted by a religious faith. This claim to neutrality is a myth. It is a myth because in making this basic assumption the non-believer is being anything but neutral or objective. He is starting from a theory which by its very nature denies that the God of Scripture can exist and therefore which denies implicitly the whole of biblical religion. Thus, his interpretation of the facts of reality will inevitably deny that the universe is what the Christian insists that it is, viz. the handiwork of God. Given his basic starting point the non-believer cannot logically come to any other conclusion.

It might be objected here that although the non-believer does not assume the existence of the God of Scripture at the outset neither does he deny it, but simply leaves it open to question. Whether God exists or not would then be determined as the result of the application of autonomous rational principles. By his own rational abilities man would thus work his way up to the knowledge of God.

However, the god of such a natural theology could not be the God revealed in Scripture, but simply a god of man's own making according to the religious fashions of the age. This is because the God of Scripture is the very foundation of all things, the source of all reason and hence of man's own rationality. Thus, as already stated, if man is to know anything truly he must think God's thoughts after him, for He is the One in terms of whom all things must be understood and measured, not the autonomous mind of man. To ask the question "does God exist?" is to assert, at the very least, that possibility lies behind God, that is to say that the concept of possibility governs the existence of God. Such a god would not be the God spoken of in Scripture for the God of Scripture is the source of all possibility. The Bible asserts that the God of whom it speaks cannot possibly not exist, and that all things depend for their existence upon Him. The God of Scripture is thus the source of all truth, the One who determines what is and what is not, and thus the One who defines all things, including man, by His creative act. To assume the autonomous rationality of man is to deny the existence of such a God. For man to claim to determine for himself whether God exists or not is to make man the source of ultimate truth, the one who determines what is and what is not, and thus the one who defines God according to his own image. Any god predicated on such grounds cannot be the God of Scripture but merely the projection of an idol onto Scripture. To question whether God exists or not is thus to deny the existence of the God of Scripture at the outset.[4]

---

4. Thus, Van Til states: "Over against this sort of god who springs from the principle of the autonomous man is the God of Scripture. He presents himself in Scripture as the One in terms of whom man himself is to forsake his autonomy and permit himself to be interpreted by God. In other words

This gives the lie to the rationalist's supposed neutrality. Modern man's so called objectivity or doctrine of neutrality is, in fact, a universal negative religious presupposition concerning the nature of reality which is held and defended by faith alone, for the assumption that the world exists and can be understood independently of the God of Scripture cannot be proved objectively any more than the existence of God can be proved objectively; it is a matter of faith.

Thus, the idea that the conflict between humanism and Christianity is one of fact versus faith, which has been promoted so much by the "scientific" establishment in our day, is a lie. The conflict is, in truth, one of faith versus faith, for there are no "brute facts" in the universe, there are only interpreted facts, and in his interpretation of the facts of reality the non-believer assumes the ability to know and understand independently of God a world which he believes exists independently of God.

It is this presupposition which governs the non-believer's thinking and hence his assessment of the facts in any and every sphere. He thus views the world around him and all things in it in terms of a theory which is pre-theoretical—i.e. unproved and by its very nature unprovable. The non-believer, therefore, begins his thinking with an act of faith in his own presuppositions about the autonomous nature of reality and his own ability as an original creative thinker and knower of the world; in other words he sees all things from a religious perspective which requires faith as its foundation.

---

the Scripture presents God as ultimate. Accordingly Scripture presents itself as the final principle by which all things must be measured. The gods produced by the thinking of man apart from Scripture are idols. To hold to any such god is to break the first commandment of the God of the Scripture." (*A Christian Theory of Knowledge* [Nutley, New Jersey: Presbyterian and Reformed Publishing Company, 1969], p. 224.)

Knowledge, faith and revelation

This is evident if we consider that there are really only two *ultimate* positions with regard to the possession of knowledge, namely, exhaustive knowledge or omniscience, and complete ignorance. If I am to know anything truly I must know everything exhaustively, otherwise what I do know, or rather what I think I know, may be affected by what I do not know, in a way and to an extent that I cannot know, and thus my "knowledge" is not knowledge in any proper sense but merely speculation. If, as a finite being who lacks exhaustive knowledge, I am to know anything truly, it must be revealed to me by one who does know all things exhaustively. On the basis of this revelation and to the extent that my reasoning is consistent with it I am then able to go on and build up my knowledge and understanding of the universe which surrounds me. But my knowledge is necessarily based on faith in the validity of this revelation.

This is so for the non-believer and for those who consider themselves to be rationalists no less than for the Christian. All knowledge, scientific or otherwise, is based on revelation, that is to say on a "given" which is pre-theoretical and thus received by faith. Such "givens" are considered axiomatic and thus assumed without question. They form the basis of all further knowledge and are therefore not susceptible of rational proof, since to question their validity would be to question the possibility of knowledge. In other words knowledge (science) hangs on faith, not faith on knowledge. The only alternative for finite human beings is total ignorance and scepticism.

The non-believer accepts the rational nature of reality as a self-evident truth. But it is a self-evident truth to man only because he is himself created in the image of the One who brought this rational cosmos into being in the first place. The rational nature of reality is revealed in the creation; it is clear for all to see, for that is how God created it.[5] The non-believer accepts the validity of this revelation as a "given," though he denies the One who made the revelation. His acceptance of it, however, is essentially a religious belief, i.e. a view of reality which is received by faith.

The non-believer further accepts, however, that the world exists and can be understood independently of the God of Scripture and that his own rational faculties are sufficient to the task of understanding that world and thus capable of giving order and meaning to the facts of reality in an original creative way. These also are fundamentally religious beliefs, that is to say presuppositions which govern the structure of the non-believer's world-view and which are received by faith alone.

To the extent that the non-believer is consistent with the former (i.e. the rational nature of reality) he is able to know the universe around him. But to the extent that he assumes the latter (i.e. the autonomous nature of reality) his knowledge is corrupted and thus false. It is the mutual exclusiveness of these basic presuppositions about the nature of reality which makes it impossible ultimately for the non-believer to construct a rationally consistent and meaningful world-view.

---

5. Van Til states the case thus: "According to Scripture, God has created the 'universe.' God has created time and space. God has created all the 'facts' of science. God has created the human mind. In this human mind God has laid the laws of thought according to which it is to operate. In the facts of science God has laid the laws of being according to which they function. In other words, the impress of God's plan is upon the whole creation.

"We may characterise this whole situation by saying that the creation of God is a revelation of God. God revealed himself in nature and God also revealed himself in the mind of man. Thus it is impossible for the mind of man to function except in an atmosphere of revelation. And every thought of man when it functioned normally in this atmosphere of revelation would express the truth as laid in the creation by God. We may therefore call a Christian epistemology a *revelational epistemology*." (*A Survey of Christian Epistemology* [Phillipsburg, New Jersey: Presbyterian and Reformed Publishing Company], p. 1.)

The circularity of reasoning

All reasoning is thus circular in that it makes certain fundamental assumptions about the nature of reality which govern the process of reasoning. These presuppositions govern both the method used to assess the data of reality and the conclusions reached about this data, since it is in terms of the validity of these presuppositions that the process of reasoning takes place. This is so for the non-believer no less than for the Christian. The world-view of the non-believer is thus based on faith, that is to say on the assumed validity of the presuppositions which govern his understanding of the nature of reality. In other words the non-believer makes certain assumptions about the world in which he lives which function essentially as religious dogmas in terms of which further knowledge and understanding of the cosmos is sought. When he denies this to be so and claims objectivity or neutrality he thereby only shows himself to be ignorant of the epistemological basis of his own thinking. He is, in a word, deluded.

Borrowed premises

However, this is not the only point at which the non-believer is deluded. Were he to be intellectually honest with himself—a rare thing indeed among the so-called scientific thinkers of our day—he would have to admit that he continually thinks and reasons in terms of totally inconsistent principles. He assumes the existence of a rationally ordered cosmos, or at least a cosmos which admits of being rationally ordered by the mind of man, which in the end comes to the same thing since if the cosmos is not rationally ordered it has no meaning and is therefore incapable of being rationally ordered—indeed, in such a universe there is no such thing as rationality. But he then attempts to construct a philosophy which is based on a concept diametrically opposed to this assumption, i.e. the total chance evolution of the universe, which means that the whole cosmos, every fact and facet of reality, including man and thus also his rationality, are mere things unrelated to each other, mere happenings, the result of chance, without meaning in relation to the other chance happenings in the universe. In other words the non-believer attempts to argue rationally about a universe which is by its nature irrational and thus incapable of being understood, for there is no basis for its intelligibility.

Van Til has described the non-believer's task as that of threading an infinite number of beads without holes onto an infinitely long string without beginning or end. But this is, in effect, precisely what the non-believer claims he has succeeded in doing, since he claims to be able to understand the world in which he lives. However, he is able to do so only to the extent that he is inconsistent with himself. In order to make any kind of sense of the universe he has to assume working principles of rationality, law, and intelligibility which fundamentally contradict his belief that the universe is the product of chaos and chance. These assumed principles are, in fact, borrowed from an understanding of reality as it has been created by God. Thus, in his use of these principles the non-believer testifies to his continual dependence upon a conception of reality which presupposes that the cosmos is the creation of the God of Scripture. Of course he denies this to be so, since to admit it would be to acknowledge God. He therefore suppresses the truth about God and continually attempts to deny the God-created nature of reality.

Thus the non-believer continually operates on borrowed premises. He has to accept the universe as God created it, viz. as a rational universe governed by law. This he is able to do, and that without being aware of it, because he is created in God's image and thus possessed of a rational nature. But as a fallen creature he denies and suppresses the truth about God and therefore attempts to explain the nature of reality in terms of a theory which presupposes the independent existence of the cosmos and the autonomous rationality of man. The result is an inconsistent epistemology which leads to many *ad hoc* theories about the origin of the universe and how it works. But because all these theories and philosophies are logically inconsistent they end in irrationality. Man cannot make sense of the universe without God. His attempts to do so are inconsistent with themselves because they are based on irreconcilable principles.

Nevertheless, because man is God's creature, created in God's image so that he should think God's thoughts after Him, in other words because he is inconsistent and assumes a world of rationality, he is able to make sense of the world around him to some extent. But he does so *in spite of* his denial of God and only to the extent that he accepts, albeit unwittingly, the God-created and God-revealed nature of reality—in other words to the extent that he does think God's thoughts after Him. Were he to be consistent with his denial of God he would have to conclude that all things are meaningless and that it is impossible to say anything intelligible about any fact or aspect of existence in the chance universe surrounding him—indeed in such a universe the concept of intelligibility is a nonsense. To an extent some schools of modern philosophy have worked out this truth more consistently than heretofore, and thus we have existentialism and nihilism.

Having your cake and eating it

The non-believer's general perspective, then, is distorted, though he is capable of individual insights and truths. These insights and truths, however, cannot be related consistently to each other nor to the unbiblical presuppositions governing his understanding of the universe. In particular, the non-believer desperately wants to keep hold of certain aspects of reality, especially qualities and facets of human personality which he knows instinctively to be essential to his own humanity, but which he is unable to account for on the basis of his own philosophy.

This has given rise to the dualistic systems of thought which have attempted to explain the nature of reality in terms of man's supposed autonomous rationality, e.g. the form-matter scheme of the ancient Greek period, the nature-grace scheme of medieval scholasticism, and the nature-freedom scheme of the Renaissance and Enlightenment period down to our own time.[6] All such philosophies are simply an attempt to have one's cake and eat it. Because they are the product of an inconsistent epistemology they are distorted and ultimately irrational, that is to say they fail to produce a rationally consistent interpretation of the universe. The non-believer is thus out of touch with reality, though he is unaware of it, and hence "intellectual schizophrenia," to use R. J. Rushdoony's term, continually manifests itself in his thinking.

The Christian view of reality

The Christian position, on the other hand, is consistent with its own presuppositions; that is to say it makes for a rationally consistent interpretation of the facts of reality. It is not schizophrenic, but is able to harmonise the whole cosmos in a unified world-view which is based on self-consistent principles. The Christian, therefore, unlike the non-believer, truly believes in a *universe*, i.e. a cosmos which is a unified entity because it finds its meaning and purpose in the creative act of the God of Scripture and thus which is intelligible and expli-

---

6. These philosophical ideas have been described by Herman Dooyeweerd in *A New Critique of Theoretical Thought* (Presbyterian and Reformed Publishing Company, 1969), *In the Twilight of Western Thought, Studies in the Pretended Autonomy of Philosophical Thought* (Nutley, New Jersey: The Craig Press, 1980), and *The Secularization of Science* cited above.

cable in terms of His word alone. Moreover, it is *only* in terms of the Christian theory of knowledge that man is able to arrive at a consistent and unified understanding of reality. The non-believer may not like the God he finds at the centre of this Christian theory of knowledge nor the nature of the world-view which it generates, but he cannot, if he is intellectually honest, deny its ultimate rationality.

Of course the non-believer will never admit this because he is a sinner, a rebel at enmity with God. He cannot therefore accept that the nature of reality is God-centred. He would rather believe a lie than bow to the God of Scripture. Ethical depravity manifests itself in every area of his life, and hence in his understanding of every aspect and fact of reality.

What has been said above is not meant to imply, however, that the Christian can never be wrong or does not make mistakes in his attempts to come to a proper understanding of the facts of reality. Obviously, the Christian does make mistakes and comes to incorrect conclusions about the world in which he lives. But he does this *in spite of* not because of his basic presuppositions about the God-created nature of reality. The difference between the believer and the non-believer is this: given his basic presuppositions about the origin and nature of reality it is impossible for the non-believer *in principle* to speak intelligibly about any fact in the universe. Because he is inconsistent with his presuppositions, however, and assumes that the universe is rationally ordered—in other words because he does his thinking in terms of pre-theoretical concepts which are borrowed from the Christian understanding of reality—he is able to arrive at a correct understanding of many aspects of the world around him. But he cannot ultimately fit these truths into a rationally consistent and meaningful world-view because his denial of God necessarily cuts him off from the one interpretive principle which is able to provide a rational foundation for such a world-view, viz. the creation of the whole cosmos *ex nihilo* by the God of Scripture.

The Christian, however, though he is capable of error in his understanding of some of the facts before him is nonetheless able to arrive at a correct understanding of the nature and meaning of reality as a whole. His world-view is *in principle* consistent with itself and with the world around him.

Application of the Christian theory of knowledge to the philosophy of education

The *sola scriptura* principle implies that the whole of life must be subjected to the will of God as revealed in the Scriptures, and at least in theory those who hold to it have always maintained that this is so. When we come to the practical application of this principle it becomes clear that the implications of the epistemology upon which it rests are far reaching. Nowhere is this more true today, and in more urgent need of our attention, than in the field of philosophy of education.

Generally speaking—though perhaps with the exception of "religious knowledge"—the non-believer will teach the same subjects and the same facts that the Christian teaches, but he will attempt to fit them into a view of reality which denies the existence of the God of Scripture and which seeks to explain all things in terms of that world-view. In such a perspective the Christian faith is merely the product of an outmoded and unscientific world-view, and thus an irrational belief system in today's scientific age. But the Christian faith is irrational in the eyes of the non-believer because it is opposed to his own religious presuppositions about the nature of reality. For the Christian the situation is exactly the reverse. The Christian's understanding of life is God-centred and therefore he seeks to understand and interpret all things in terms of the creative purpose of the God of Scripture and the word He has given to govern man's life. Because He is the Creator and sustainer of all things the universe finds its purpose and meaning only in Him. Thus the denial of God is a leap into irrationality and intellectual suicide.

This sets the issue of education in its philosophical context. These two positions are mutually exclusive. They can never agree fundamentally on the interpretation of the facts of reality at *any* point if they are consistent with their presuppositions. For the Christian and the humanist, therefore, there can be no common ground.[7] This truth has been understood more by the humanists heretofore than it has by Christians. It is the mutual exclusiveness of these two positions which makes the provision of a specifically Christian education for our children essential, and the sending of our children to state schools to be educated by humanists a denial of the faith implicitly.

This truth—that it is the nature of our basic religious presuppositions which governs our understanding of all things—is thus the fundamental rationale behind a specifically Christian philosophy and practice of education, since if it is true that the only valid interpretation of the world in which we live is that which is based on God's revealed word, then the education we give our children must be based on that word at all points. A Christian education, therefore, is one which enables

---

7. Common ground must not be confused with common grace. Because of God's common grace to mankind the non-believer does understand to a degree the world in which he lives and is able to arrive at the truth concerning many aspects of reality. But, as I have argued above, this is *in spite of* rather than because of the basic presuppositions governing his thinking. In other words the non-believer is inconsistent with his own epistemology, and the reason for this is that he is created in God's image and is unable to deny or deface that image totally. Indeed, it is only because of his creation in the image of God that the non-believer is able to function as a rational human being, even when he uses all his powers as a rational being to deny his creator—that is, when he attempts to use rational arguments to deny the existence of the God of Scripture. The fact that the image of God in man has not been totally obliterated by the fall, and thus the fact that the non-believer is still able to arrive at a degree of truth concerning the world in which he lives, is an aspect of God's common grace to mankind, but it does not mean that there is, in terms of a consistent epistemology on either part, any common ground between the believer and the non-believer concerning any aspect or fact of reality.

the student to think God's thoughts after Him in every discipline and area of life; in other words one which provides him with both a conceptual framework based on and consistent with the definitive interpretation of reality set forth in God's word and the intellectual tools to assimilate the data of reality into that framework. Only such an education will enable the student to make ultimate sense of the world in which he lives and equip him to fulfil his cultural mandate to bring all things into subjection to Christ.

Furthermore, because the Christian believes that all things were created by God and therefore that the facts of reality can only be understood properly in terms of God's creative purpose, the Christian philosophy of education emphatically denies that any discipline or field of study, any scientific method, or the findings and conclusions of the investigation of any and every facet of the cosmos, can be neutral with regard to the fundamental presuppositions of the epistemology on which it is based. It is God's creative act which gives meaning to the data of reality and thus the only theory that can speak with authority about or make ultimate sense of this data is that which presupposes the God of Scripture as the fundamental principle of interpretation of all things: "For from Him and through Him and to Him are all things" (Rom. 11:36) and "He is before all things, and in Him all things hold together" (Col. 1:17). This truth is the beginning of all knowledge, for only in terms of this truth is true knowledge possible. Thus "the fear of the Lord is the beginning of knowledge" (Pr. 1:7).

It is thus treason against God to hand our children over to non-believers for the formation of their intellectual outlook and philosophy of life—for that is what the child is given in school, viz. a total world-view, not simply specialised or technical information on certain subjects which their parents are unable to provide; indeed, a complete philosophy of life is precisely what most educators pride themselves on providing. Anyone who supposes that he can maintain control over the kind of world-view that his children imbibe while sending them to a state or humanist school is deluded. It is impossible to undo five days of systematic instruction in the humanist world-view with one morning of Sunday school, which is usually all that the children of Christians get by way of a specifically Christian education—and even this is usually of a very poor quality and limited to "religious education" in the narrow sense. We are denying the faith when we hand our children over to be educated by our enemies, to be instructed and encouraged to view the world and all things in it in terms of the godless categories of human thought. To do so is to dedicate our children to another god. It is idolatry and treason all rolled into one.

Conclusion

I began this chapter by claiming that modern Protestant theology has abandoned the *sola scriptura* basis on which it was originally founded, and that this has happened because the epistemological basis upon which it rested has been abandoned. This has not been done self-consciously, however, and this is because, by and large, the epistemological basis of the *sola scriptura* conception of theology was not held self-consciously by those who adhered to the *sola scriptura* principle. It was assumed theologically but not self-consciously. Hence Van Til criticises those who held to the *sola scriptura* principle but who, nevertheless, attempted to construct an apologetics which was based on a common ground rationalistic epistemology—e.g. Hodge, Warfield and the old Princetonians. This, according to Van Til, gives too much away; indeed, it surrenders all *in principle* to the enemy. With the rise of rationalistic humanism and its claim to scientific method etc. many have concluded that the gospel is no longer intellectually defensible—at least the kind of gospel held by the Reformers with their belief in the Scriptures as the infallible word of the living God and the supreme and binding authority in all matters of belief and conduct.

Thus, without sure ground to stand upon when forced to defend the faith, the Protestant church, including the evangelical wing, has broken ranks and fled before an enemy whose strength lies only in an illusion of rationality. Some, embarrassed by the claims of Scripture and unwilling to sacrifice intellectual respectability in an academic world hostile to biblical truth, have frantically sought to find ways of showing that the Scriptures really meant all along what today's "scientific" rationalists are saying—witness the gap theory of creation and the idea of theistic evolution, which was developed to fit in with a theory which is not only unbiblical but untenable in terms of any proper conception of the scientific method. In this process of accommodation, however, Protestant theology has ceased to be essentially scriptural in any honest and meaningful sense, and has moved towards a form of natural theology which is more acceptable in the contemporary intellectual and academic climate. Others, wishing to claim adherence to biblical faith and unwilling to adopt a rationalistic theology, have escaped unwittingly into the very cage that the rationalists have built for them, viz. a faith-reason dichotomy between the Christian religion and so-called scientific or empirical truth. Both of these trends are the result of giving too much credence to the illegitimate claims of rationalistic philosophy. In short, the Protestant church today is suffering from a severe attack of intellectual cowardice in the face of the enemy.

If the church is to recover from this condition and reclaim lost ground it must throw off its intellectual bondage to the rationalistic perspective of modern philosophy and theology and return again to the *sola scriptura* conception of the Christian faith. Our task then is to re-build a consistent theology in terms of that principle and develop a hermeneutic which is capable of applying Scripture to the contemporary world, thus releasing the command word of God into the life of the church and into the world we have been commissioned to bring under the discipline of Christ.

If we are to communicate biblical truth effectively, however, our apologetics must be based on an epistemology which is rationally consistent with itself and with our understanding of Scripture as the infallible and authoritative revelation of God and of His will for man. On such a basis we can confidently challenge all the rationalistic philosophy and systems of thought arrayed against the Christian religion in our day. In so doing, however, we must make it clear that the Christian epistemology on which we build is not merely a rational foundation for the truth we proclaim, it is the only rational foundation for *any* claim to truth. It is the basis not only of scriptural truth, but of all truth, whether religiously or scientifically conceived, for the claims of biblical truth are all embracing. Only on the basis of such an epistemology are we in a position to reveal the intellectual idolatry of disbelief and expose to the non-believer the irrationality of his own position.

2

EDUCATION AND IDOLATRY

In the perspective of the non-believer discussed in the previous chapter it is clear that man's rationality and creative genius are not derived from nor in any way dependent upon any source outside of himself, but are original autonomous qualities of human personality. Hence man defines both his own nature and the nature of the world in which he lives, and he understands all things in terms of himself. Man is the ultimate reference point for every fact in the universe which surrounds him. Thus, in a revealing passage by Karl Popper we are told:

> Copernicus deprived man of his central position in the physical universe. Kant's Copernican Revolution takes the sting out of this. He shows us not only that our location in the physical universe is irrelevant, but also that in a sense our universe may well be said to turn about us; for it is we who produce, at least in part, the order we find in it; it is we who create our knowledge of it. We are discoverers: and discovery is a creative art.[1]

This is, of course, the oldest of all heresies, going right back to the fall of man in the Garden of Eden. Adam would define the nature of reality and of his own being and determine for himself his place in the order of things according to his own autonomous rationality. Of course this meant also

1. Karl Popper, *Conjectures and Refutations, The Growth of Scientific Knowledge* (London and Henley: Routledge and Kegan Paul, [1963] 1972), p. 181.

that the Creator God Himself now had to be defined according to the image of man, since Adam had made his own rationality the touchstone of all truth, meaning and purpose. This process of reasoning is graphically illustrated by the philosophy of Immanuel Kant, which is basic to much of modern thought. The following passage is taken from Kant's *Religion within the Limits of Pure Reason,* a title which in itself reveals much about the idolatry implicit in idealistic and rationalistic humanism:

> Much as my words may startle you, you must not condemn me for saying: every man creates his God. From the moral point of view . . . you even *have* to create your God, in order to worship in Him your creator. For in whatever way . . . the Deity should be made known to you, and even . . . if He should reveal Himself to you: it is you . . . who must judge whether you are permitted [by your conscience] to believe in Him, and to worship Him.[2]

A more striking recapitulation of the rationale for Adam's original sin could hardly be found. Simply put this means that man is his own god, for one's god is always that in which one places ultimate authority. According to Popper "The spirit of Kant's ethics may well be summed up in these words: dare to be free; and respect the freedom of others."[3] The spirit of Kant's ethics may equally well be summed up in these words: dare to be as God, knowing good and evil for yourself (Gen. 3:5). The ethics of Kant is the ethics of rebellion.

This philosophy of man as god—humanism—will work itself out in one of two ways: either through libertarianism and thence to anarchy, or through a statist view of man and society and thence to totalitarianism.[4] Both ideologies are very much

---

2. Cited in *ibid.*, p. 182.
3. *Ibid.*
4. For the philosophy behind this polarisation see R. J. Rushdoony, *The One and the Many, Studies in the Philosophy of Order and Ultimacy* (Fairfax, Virginia: Thoburn Press, 1978).

with us today and at work in educational theory and practice in our land, and have been for a long time. However, it is the latter which primarily concerns us here since statist ideology not only poses a threat, via the Local Education Authorities, to the authority of parents in their endeavours to give their children a godly education, but can also exert great psychological pressure upon Christian parents to conform to the status quo which has been established over the last century through the tax funding of state education. It is important, therefore, that we understand this ideology and expose the idolatrous nature of the philosophy underpinning it.

The statist view of man

As we have seen, for humanism man is at the centre of his world. But there are many individual men and the ideal of man cannot be limited to the idiosyncrasies of any one particular human being. Thus, for statist humanism the ideal of man is always beyond man in particular and is embodied instead in the concept of society. In this perspective it is the *idea* of society and of man as a *social creature* which is idolised. But this idea of society is far removed from the world of real men and the needs and concerns of real men. This is because the ideal is always beyond the historical situation. This abstract idea of society must, therefore, if it is to become a reality in history, be embodied in some representative organ or institution on earth which then moulds the historical situation and attempts to bring it into conformity with the ideal. This institution—the perfect embodiment or true expression of the idea of human society as understood by statist humanism—is the state. Hence the state is "the Divine Idea as it exists on earth," to use Hegel's phrase.

Since in the ideology of statism man is the creature of society—that is to say he is what he is as a result of social conditioning—it is the duty of the state to determine and regulate all the parameters and variables within man's social and cultural matrix so that the end product conforms to the ideal of the perfect social being. In other words, as the abstract idea of society incarnate in history it is the state's purpose to re-create society in its own image. As the head and guardian of society the state must care for, mould, and discipline in terms of its own purpose those who will constitute the society of the future. It is not surprising therefore that the family is depreciated by statists and control of the infant from birth seen more and more as a state responsibility. The child is the creature of the state and society is his true family. Hence, should the child's genetic family prove a hindrance to his development into an ideal member of the statist society its custodianship of the child must be suspended.

This is not mere theory. While it may not be as obvious in Britain as the above analysis suggests, this ideology is subtly at work in our land, and can be seen in a more conspicuous form in advanced socialist countries such as Sweden. We have perhaps an indication of things to come in the current attempts of some to prohibit by law all forms of corporal punishment of children by their parents.

In this perspective man is defined by the state as a social creature. The individual is nothing except in relation to society since his growth and development as a personality are determined and controlled by his social environment. Thus education is necessarily a process of maturation into the image of man as defined by the state. The goal of education is therefore integration into society. Hence we often hear educators speaking of the child's development in terms of his eventual usefulness as a full participating member of society. It is common also to hear politicians speaking in such terms. A man or woman is considered mature and valuable to society because he or she is a useful member thereof and able to contribute something worthwhile to the community. The individual only truly realises himself to the extent that he helps to realise the ideal society which he exists to serve.

It is to be expected ultimately that those who are unable or unwilling to meet this expectation be denied the status of human beings and either exiled in psychiatric hospitals and labour camps, where they can be forced to serve the state as slaves, or, if they are unable to do even this, put to death. Such practices have been common in Soviet countries for many years, and were of course a feature of the Nazi regime. Some of them are now common in the West, for example abortion of deformed foetuses, or even of a perfectly formed foetus if the birth of a child is going to lead to "hardship" or "mental illness" for the mother. The addition of genetic engineering to man's arsenal of social control techniques presents a bleak prospect for man's future under such an ideology.

The statist philosophy of education

With regard to education, however, it is clear that our definition of man determines the nature of our educational philosophy. It also determines the method and goal of the educational process. For the humanist education is necessarily man-centred. Man is the measure of himself and all things. The goal of education is for man to realise himself in terms of the image of his god, whether that god is his own personal ego, as with libertarianism, or the statist ideal of society or of man as a social creature. For the libertarian the process will be geared to the individual and his needs, desires and aspirations at all points. For the statist it will be geared to man's social environment. The purpose of education therefore is to equip the child to take his place in adult society by fully integrating him into the peer group. The peer group is thus the reference point for the child's development at every stage in his education.

For statists the lack of such an education is considered a deprivation, and to deliberately withdraw the child from this process of assimilation into the group is an act of cruelty. Hence, although it must be acknowledged that the statist eradication of all forms of private schooling is in practice to a great extent motivated by envy and hatred of privilege, it is, nonetheless, logically consistent with statist ideology to seek to eradicate from society all those educational institutions which fail to provide an education which is thoroughly integrated into statist educational philosophy and practice, which of course ultimately means state funding and control. To be outside the social norm as defined by socialist ideology is an aberration which can only be seen as detrimental to the child and society alike.

Thus the methodology of statist education requires first and foremostly integration of the child into the peer group. Without this, education is meaningless for socialist philosophy. Education is primarily a process of initiation or baptism into the society in which the child will ultimately find his vocation and which will define his existence as an adult. I use the word baptism here quite deliberately because of its religious connotation, for the principle of assimilation into the peer group is a dogma which is held tenaciously by the followers of statist educational theory, which is at heart a religious faith in an idolatrous conception of mankind.

This humanistic faith exerts a strong influence on many Christian parents who have been misled and manipulated into believing that unless their children are forced to integrate into the pagan social environment of their peer group they will become inadequate, withdrawn and anti-social members of society. Indeed, it has been claimed that unless the children of Christians are thus integrated with their peers they will most likely turn out to be schizophrenic and even malevolent individuals. Such talk can exert a powerful psychological influence on Christian parents who are considering withdrawing their children from the state school in order to provide them with a godly education. The implication is that to educate the child outside of the established system is child abuse.

It is vitally important therefore that Christian parents understand the religious perspective underpinning such views. In socialist ideology, no less than in Christianity or indeed any other religion, man is defined by his god, which for socialism is the state, and the purpose of education is therefore to promote maturation into the image of man as a social creature. In other words the state is the god incarnate in whose image man is to re-create himself. Education is the process by which this re-creation is to be accomplished.

The Christian perspective

The Christian, however, starts—or at least ought to start—from a totally different perspective. It is the God of Scripture who has created and therefore who defines man; and He has created man in *His own* image. The aim of education is thus to promote maturation in the image of *God*, and it is the duty of Christian parents to care for the child, mould his character, and discipline him in terms of *God's* purpose for his life.

According to the Westminster Shorter Catechism "Man's chief end is to glorify God, and to enjoy Him forever," and "God created man male and female, after his own image, in knowledge, righteousness, and holiness, with dominion over the creatures." The purpose of a Christian education is therefore to enable the child to shoulder the responsibilities and privileges of being God's image bearer, and to equip him for a life of service to God as His vicegerent on earth. Since it is God who defines man, not society or the state, the role of the peer group and the process of socialisation will not be of primary importance. Society, as a group of individuals holding certain things in common and sharing a common mode of life, is itself a *subsidiary* aspect of the human condition, for Adam originally was alone as a human being. He was not, however, on that account any the less human, for his humanity consisted in his being God's image bearer. Everything which sets man apart from the animals and thus which constitutes his humanity is to be found in the fact that he is created in the image of God. Man's need for communion or fellowship is also primarily related to the fact that he bears God's image, for in the Godhead there is communion between the persons of the Trinity. Thus man, as a dependent creature bearing God's image, stands in need of communion also. But—and this is the point which is of fundamental importance here—since man is God's creature and the bearer of His image his need for communion consists first and foremostly in the need for communion with *God*, not man. As God's image bearer Adam stood in a covenant relation to God before he stood in relation to any other human being. It was his position in relation to God as His image bearer, not man, which constituted his humanity, for Adam was created alone as the first human being *before* Eve was created.

The communion of man with man, or society, is thus a derivative of the human condition, not its defining feature. The existence of community and of covenant relations between men is the result of the fact that man is a covenantal creature by nature, created in God's image for communion with Him. In other words man was indeed created for fellowship, but for fellowship with God first of all, and with man secondarily.

This is clearly demonstrated by the fact that when this communion with God is broken man's communion with his fellow creatures disintegrates also. Our times demonstrate this very well in many ways. An obvious example is the amazing divorce rate today in the West. In this connection R. J. Rushdoony has drawn attention to the fact that one of the key concepts in our age of psychoanalysis is "alienation,"[5] the breakdown of community and communication between men. Since it is God who defines man, human society correctly consti-

5. *Ibid.*, p. 368.

tuted is a group of people covenanted or in communion together *under God.* The community which rejects this definition of society and seeks to order its life independently of God's word will not ultimately stand nor endure in history. Thus, approximately twenty-one civilisations have risen and perished in the course of history, and Western civilisation is now in the process of decline also, for it has rejected the One who alone is able to provide man with a true basis for social cohesion and long-term cultural stability. Men cannot ultimately achieve lasting communion with each other on any basis other than communion with God. This is because as God's image bearer communion with God is of primary importance for man, and therefore the only stable foundation for true communion between men.

Of course, being able to associate and work with others is an important part of the child's growth and development, and we should not deny this. But we must understand that the reference point for every aspect of our social life no less than for our personal devotional life, is God and our covenant and communion with Him, not our fellow man. As Christians we regulate our behaviour with both believers and non-believers according to God's word, for our communion with others, if it is to be communion in any meaningful sense, must be based on the fact that we share a common nature which is created in the image of God.

Were this not true man's relationship with his fellow humans would be no different to the relationships which exist between animals. Man's need for fellowship and communion, however, is more than the need for biological union for the sake of self-preservation and preservation of the species. There are indeed many animal societies which work admirably on a biological and instinctual level. But that is where they stop. Man's need for communion and society is above this; it is not merely animal in nature but is based on the need for communion with others who bear God's image. The existence of human society, therefore, is not primarily a biological fact, but a *spiritual* fact, that is to say based on the communicable attributes of God. And for this reason human society is subordinate to and derived from man's capacity for communion with God.

Of course it is true that God created man male *and* female (Gen. 1:27), and that man was not meant to exist entirely on his own as a human being. When Adam had named all the animals there was still not found a helper suitable for him, and therefore God created Eve to be his wife (Gen. 2:21-23). What has been said above is not intended to depreciate or minimise the importance and value of human society and it is recognised that mankind ordinarily finds the fulfilment of his being and calling as God's image bearer, and hence glorifies God truly, in the setting of human companionship. Thus we are told that "The Lord God said, 'It is not good for man to be alone; I will make him a helper suitable for him'" (Gen. 2:18). Marriage, family life and society generally are expressions of important aspects of man's nature. Human society is a God-created fact of life which must not be denied.

My intention is simply to stress two important points: *first*, that human society does not *define* mankind, that is to say it is not what makes man human. For the Christian it is the fact that man is created in the image of God that makes him human, whereas for the socialist, man is defined by *society*—i.e. he finds his nature, meaning and purpose in relation to the society of which he is a part and which he exists to serve in one form or another. *Secondly*, human society, if it is to be truly human and thus meaningful, that is to say if it is to be the communion and companionship that God intended it to be, must be based on the prior necessity of communion with God, since this communion with God is essential to the proper expression of human life, and hence of human companionship and society, which is an aspect of human life.

The religious nature of education

Thus, our definition of man—what he is, where he comes from, what the purpose of his existence is etc.—is the determining factor in our understanding of what education is and governs both the aims of education and the methods used to achieve those aims. For the non-believer no less than for the Christian, therefore, the meaning, method and goal of education is based inescapably on metaphysical—i.e. religious—presuppositions about the nature of man. For the Christian, education is necessarily a process of maturation in the image of God, for this is precisely the purpose for which man was created, viz. to image God on earth. Thus the peer group is a secondary factor in education, and the process of socialisation must always be seen in the light of man's higher calling to image and glorify God on earth. Man's first allegiance is to God. It is vitally important that Christian parents realise this and refuse to bow down to an idolatrous notion of the primacy of the peer group. God has created and defined man in His own image and we are to nurture and educate our children in conformity to His image, not that of apostate men.

Our concern for social integration, provided it is seen in a secondary place and is subject to the necessity of obedience to God's word, is of course a valid concern. But sending our children to be integrated into the pagan image of man by subjecting them to peer group pressure is not the answer to the valid concerns that Christian parents might have about their children being educated at home without the same degree of contact with other children that the average non-believer has. This is not to say that Christian children should not mix or play with non-believing children. But it is to say that they should not be *educated* as non-believers, and that is precisely what will happen if they are educated in state schools—or pagan private schools.

Furthermore, it should be said that it is precisely because the Christian sees man's need for communion first and foremostly as the need for communion with God, and precisely because he sees education in the light of this principle, that those children who are educated at home or in Christian schools in terms of this Christian philosophy so often turn out to be the ones who are more able to function as responsible members of society. Such children are generally more mature, both intellectually and in terms of character and general competence, than the average member of the pagan peer group. Christian children thus educated are a stable element in society since they are generally more well balanced and have in their faith a true basis for social cohesion. It is simply not true that such an education produces inward looking, inadequate individuals. On the contrary, not only do such children usually achieve consistently better academic results and prove to be generally more mature and able to mix socially, but their ability to socialise is often at a higher level and related more to the adult world.

The guiding principle in education: maturity versus immaturity

This last point, however, is likely to bring out a salient feature of the prevailing mentality of our age, especially in its expectations of children. Because the non-believer does not see man as God's creature, created originally as a mature human being, he does not set the same premium on maturity.[6] The responsibilities of maturity are burdens which he seeks to avoid. Men seek instead a life of leisure and play without responsibility. One can see this so clearly in the kind of advertising that is common today. Products are advertised by conjur-

---

6. R. J. Rushdoony, *Revolt Against Maturity, A Biblical Psychology of Man* (Fairfax, Virginia: Thoburn Press, 1977), p. 6f.

ing up images of a burden-free life style in which the responsibilities of reality are conspicuous by their absence. The desire to escape from responsibility characterises much of our modern world. This mentality produces an infantile culture, since at its root is the desire to remain as a child, without responsibility and dependent in all things.[7] For this kind of mentality staying young, both physically and intellectually, is a major occupation and goal in life. Indeed childhood is often seen as a kind of paradise or Garden of Eden. Growing up is thus the loss of innocence, a kind of humanistic version of the fall. It is this mentality which is the source of the "pop" culture which dominates so much of modern Western society.

Obviously, in such an ethos the early development of the child is not prized. Children must not be allowed or encouraged to "grow up before their time." To deny a child the unfettered enjoyment of his childhood by encouraging early development and a mature attitude to the adult world is often seen as a great evil. Children who do mature early and whose achievements are ahead of their peer group are considered precocious and labelled "overachievers" by socialist educators. Such children are seen as outside the parameters of what constitutes normality. Since normality is defined by the group and the purpose of education is to enable the child to fit into the group such "overachieving" is undesirable.

In fact it could be argued that a more likely result of making the peer group the dominant factor in education is to

---

7. This mentality has also played a large part in the growth of socialism and statism generally since it is by promising such a lifestyle that socialist politicians recruit their voters. Salvation by politics, in which the proletariat is delivered from the responsibilities and burdens of life by the state bureaucracy is a basic driving force in socialist ideology. In such a perspective responsibility equals evil and "social justice"—the socialist version of salvation—is in part deliverance from the problems and demands of adult life. Socialists fail to understand, however, that freedom without responsibility is a pure dream, and that the real consequence of the abdication of responsibility to the state is *slavery*.

produce immature individuals who are unable to cope with the responsibilities and burdens of adult life and hence dependent both psychologically and, in the end, materially on the paternalistic state; in other words that it tends to produce people who are incapable of being free in any meaningful sense of the word. The fact that our society faces this problem of dependence in large measure today should at the very least give us reason enough to review critically the ideal of social integration which undergirds current educational philosophy and which is assumed so often to be the correct pattern for the development of the child.

To set a premium on maturity, however, produces a culture characterised by progress across the whole spectrum of human life and activity. Christianity emphasises man's duty to God and his responsibilities as a mature creature created in God's image "in knowledge, righteousness, and holiness, with dominion over the creatures" (Westminster Shorter Catechism, Q. 10, *A.*). It produces, therefore, a mature culture which sets a premium on freedom and dominion *in Christ*, not play and escape from reality. It is no accident that it is the Western world—Christendom, with all its faults and failures—which alone has given us the kind of cultural, scientific and economic progress which has made the modern world possible, and a more humane and civilised world in which to live.

Conclusion

As Christians we must reject the pagan outlook. The purpose of a Christian education is to enable the child to grow in the image of God into a mature adult, to equip him to shoulder his responsibilities as God's image bearer, and provide him with the tools to fulfil his creation mandate to extend his dominion over the earth as God's vicegerent. This is the purpose of man's existence and an education which is not geared to enabling the child to fulfil this purpose is a failure, for it withholds him from his development into a mature human being. We are not at liberty, as Christians, to subject our children to an education which baptises them into the godless image of fallen man. Man's humanity consists in his being the bearer of God's image, and it is this image which is of primary importance and the reference point in the child's education at every level. Christian parents need to reassess their understanding of priorities here. When the biblical priorities are reasserted in educational theory and practice the child will benefit and mature more quickly in terms of God's purpose, thereby enabling him to play his part in society *for the glory of God.*

3

EDUCATION AS AN ASPECT OF THE COVENANT

There is a strong educational emphasis running throughout the whole of Scripture. For instance, the people of God are constantly commanded and encouraged to learn and meditate upon the law (Deut. 11:18-21, Ps. 1:2, 94:12). Indeed, the law is itself in the most fundamental sense a body of teaching, an educational curriculum in godliness for every area of life—the word *torah* means literally "direction" or "instruction."

Consider also the place of history in the Bible. The teaching of history is seen as a vitally important parental duty (Deut. 4:7-9, 6:20-25), and the history books in both Old and New Testaments form a considerable part of holy Scripture. Indeed, the biblical philosophy of history in its widest sense is basic to the concept of progress and has been of fundamental importance in the rise of Western civilisation. It has been argued that it is the biblical concept of linear time, in contrast to the pagan idea of cyclical time, which has been responsible for the emergence of scientific progress in the Western world.[1]

---

1. Stanley L. Jaki, *Science and Creation, From eternal cycles to an oscillating universe* (Edinburgh: Scottish Academic Press). However, the concept of linear time is not to be seen as the only distinctively biblical concept which was necessary for the development of modern science. In effect it forms a necessary intellectual precondition for the efforts of man to develop and control the natural world. Along with the concept of linear time the biblical doctrines of the cultural mandate and the validity of man's dominion over the earth have been of equal importance. Both of these concepts are peculiarly

Then there is the wisdom literature, which is dedicated exclusively to education. The book of Proverbs was written to give instruction in wisdom, justice, judgement and equity, to give subtlety to the simple and knowledge and discretion to the young, so that the wise may increase in learning and the learned attain wisdom (Pr. 1:3-5).

Likewise, in the New Testament the epistles are largely educational in emphasis. Indeed the whole Bible is concerned with education. God has spoken to man by means of His word and we are to understand and apply that word to our lives, and teach our children to do the same. Thus the apostle Paul commends and bears witness to the validity and effectiveness of Timothy's Christian education: "continue in the things you have learned and become convinced of, knowing from whom you have learned them; and that from childhood you have known the sacred writings which are able to give you the wisdom that leads to salvation through faith which is in Christ Jesus. All Scripture is inspired by God and profitable for teaching, for reproof, for correction, for training in righteousness; that the man of God may be adequate, equipped for every good work" (2 Tim. 3:14-17). So often we turn to this passage simply as a proof text for the doctrine of infallibility and miss its significance for the biblical philosophy of education. God has given us the Scriptures that we might be truly and properly educated in terms of His purpose, and thus equipped to fulfil our vocation as God's people.

---

biblical concepts and this is pre-eminently the reason that scientific progress has been the product of a specifically Christian cultural matrix and has accompanied the spread of Christian civilisation. In contrast to this biblical emphasis on legitimate dominion advancing over time towards a definite result is paganism, in which man attempts to better his conditions in life either by seeking illegitimate domination over others through the use of force, e.g. Fascism and Communism, or through the control of the spiritual world by means of magic, e.g. animism, Hinduism etc. These two differing approaches to man's condition produce radically different civilisations, the general characteristics of which can be seen by contrasting the First and Third World societies.

It was the responsibility and destiny of Israel, as a nation which possessed the "oracles of God," to be a "guide to the blind, a light to those who are in darkness, a corrector of the foolish, a teacher of the immature," since they had in their law the "embodiment of knowledge and of the truth" (Rom. 2:19-20). And this is certainly no less the calling of the Christian church today. Thus, missionaries to pagan nations establish schools as one of the most important of their tasks. They take non-believers from their heathen cultures and re-educate them. They give their children a Christian education instead of a pagan education. Missionary work is more than simply establishing churches in far off lands. It is the task of converting a whole culture, a total way of life, to the Christian religion. Missionary work is an example to us here. We must see the logic of this and apply it to our own increasingly secular—and thus pagan—situation. It is as necessary to establish specifically Christian schools in our own land as it is in darkest Africa, and for the same reason, namely, that Christ demands our whole life, our whole culture, to be subjected to His authority.

Obviously such a task requires an educated people. The Jews had in their law true knowledge and wisdom, and they were *required* to educate their children consistently in terms of their faith. Thus the law states: "And these words, which I am commanding you today, shall be on your heart; and you shall teach them diligently to your sons and shall talk of them when you sit in your house and when you walk by the way and when you lie down and when you rise up" (Deut. 6:6-7, cf. 11:18-21). Education was to be a consistent and continual process. To fail to provide one's children with a godly education was thus to neglect one's parental responsibilities under the covenant.

The social and cultural context

We must now turn to consider more closely what the Bible

has to say about the responsibilities of parents with regard to the education of their children. In so doing, however, we must bear in mind that there are considerable cultural differences between the kind of society represented in the biblical record and our own society.

These differences are particularly evident in the degree of institutional forms developed in our own culture for the provision of many social needs. Indeed, institutional differentiation is a particular characteristic of our society. In contrast there is in the biblical society far less institutional differentiation across the whole spectrum of social life. It may appear at first sight, therefore, that a particular need such as education is not adequately provided for because we do not see in the biblical society the existence of a separate institution dedicated solely to its provision.

This is a judgement that we are particularly likely to make because we tend to look back at more primitive cultures with a modern perspective and assess them in terms of our own highly differentiated and bureaucratic social arrangements, often assuming without good reason that the latter are necessarily superior. However, the lack of a specific institution dedicated solely to education does not in itself imply a lack of provision in the biblical society, nor does it necessarily mean that we are more enlightened today and that the biblical arrangement for the provision of education was inferior to our own. On the contrary, with regard to education the biblical model should be seen as having permanent validity and thus the correct Christian model for today. Therefore, in this specific area, as in so many others, a return to the biblical model would be a considerable improvement on the highly institutionalised and bureaucratic arrangement which is mistakenly taken for a great achievement today.

Nevertheless, because of these institutional differences between our own society and the biblical society, we often fail to appreciate the full impact of the biblical teaching on this subject. We must recognise, therefore, that in contrast to our own institutionally organised society biblical society is organised on a highly *covenantal* basis. This meant that education, like every other area of life, found its context in the covenantal structure of life. By the nature of the case the biblical society did not require a highly differentiated or distinctively institutionalised social structure in order for parents to provide their children with a covenantally faithful education. If we approach the biblical teaching on education with an alien perspective which assumes that an adequate education necessitates such an arrangement, which is essentially a modern idea, we shall likely miss the significance of what the Bible has to say on the subject. In order to appreciate biblical educational norms, therefore, we need to reorientate ourselves to the covenantal perspective set forth in God's word.

The covenantal perspective

In the previous chapter reference was made to the fact that there is a community of persons within the Godhead. Each member of the Trinity is in communion with the other members of the Trinity. Since man is created in God's image he also reflects this aspect of God's nature. The need for communion is thus a basic characteristic of human nature. But unlike God, who is an aseity,—a totally self-contained and independent reality, uncreated and eternal—man is a being dependent upon his Creator in all things and thus, as stated above, his need for communion is realised first and foremostly in communion with God.

The nature of the relationship which exists between God and man is expressed in Scripture by the concept of *covenant*. God relates to man by means of a covenant and there can be no communion between God and man except on the basis of this covenant. The covenant defines the relationship that exists between God as the Creator and man as His creature and image bearer.

Furthermore, it is important to grasp the fact that this covenant relation is the consequence of man's creation as a dependent being in God's image and thus an inescapable fact of life, not a take it or leave it option for those with a religious disposition. The covenant is inextricably bound up with man's nature as a being made in the image of God, for the communion which exists between God and man is a reflection of the eternal communion which exists between the members of the Trinity.

The creaturely and dependent nature of man's relation to God, and the sovereign nature of God's relation to man, is expressed by the structure of the covenant that God has established with mankind. In this covenant the Lord God, as man's Creator and Sovereign, establishes His authority over His creature and thus defines the limits of man's life according to His sovereign will. Man, as God's creature, stands under that authority in the relation of a subject to his sovereign. The terms of the covenant promise salvation and the blessings of communion with God and enjoin faithfulness and obedience on man's part. The scope of the covenant is comprehensive, embracing the whole of man's life. It defines man's calling as God's vicegerent and prescribes the terms of his creation mandate to establish his dominion over the earth. In other words, the covenant is not to be construed as a limited or incidental contract established as a means to a particular end, but rather as a total way of life by which man is to love and serve his Creator.[2] The covenant is thus the supreme fact of life for man, the discarding of which constitutes the whole of man's fall into sin, and restoration into covenant fellowship with God, the whole of salvation.

When Adam sinned against God in the Garden he broke the covenant and fell from his standing as one who lived in

---

2. Herman Hoeksema, *Reformed Dogmatics* (Grand Rapids: Reformed Free Publishing Association), p. 222.

communion with God. In Adam the whole human race fell also, since he was the federal head and representative of humanity. However, God has re-established man's standing with Himself by means of a perfect blood sacrifice, offered by Jesus Christ at Calvary, as the propitiation for sin. By faith the people of God in times past had access to this redemption in Jesus Christ, which was typified in the sacrificial rituals of the Old Testament ceremonial law, and were thus restored to covenant fellowship with God. Having thus redeemed His people God revealed His law to them as a guide and rule of life. This law constitutes the terms of the covenant under which God has redeemed His people, and it gives direction and regulation for every area of life. The life of the whole community of God's people was therefore covenantally structured; that is to say it was a Theocracy. In other words, the terms (law) of the covenant established at every level the nature and basic form of the social structure through which the people of God lived out the life of faith and obedience.

The place and responsibility of the family in the covenant

In this social structure the place of the family is of fundamental importance. The family is the basic and primary social unit through which the covenant life of the community is realised. It functioned as the basic economic and educational unit as well as providing for the welfare of its members. These three areas of family responsibility—welfare, economy and education—form the basic elements of what has been called the "trustee family."

The trustee family is the concept of the family set forth in the Bible. According to R. J. Rushdoony: "The Biblical family can be compared to a corporation. A corporation differs, in that it is an artificial legal person and is created by the state. A corporation does not die when its founders die, or when its officers die; it continues to exist legally apart from its stockholders, who continue, as long as they are alive to draw dividends from it. Similarly, the family is a corporation, consisting of parents and children. It pays out dividends to the children in care, support, and inheritance, and it returns dividends to the parents in care and support as needed. As a corporation, it administers its properties and income in terms of its ordained and God-given purpose. For this reason, no arbitrary or purely personal decisions can govern the decisions of members of the corporation; they are both individual persons and a corporate entity, and their truest function is in terms of a full consideration of both offices under God."[3]

The idea of the Welfare State, in which these God-ordained areas of family responsibility are provided for by the state, is clearly therefore unbiblical and anti-covenantal. The Welfare State is a frontal attack on the biblical doctrine of the family, for it destroys precisely those areas of the family's authority which enable it to function as the trustee of its economic resources with responsibility for the welfare and education of its members. "For the state to enter into the control of either children or property is to transgress on the sphere of the family and to claim to be that corporation whose life is the care of the family. Such a claim is a major transgression against God's law-order."[4]

Under socialism the family is really a redundant and outmoded form of life. The state is the trustee of society in all areas, and thus in effect claims to be the individual's only true family. The biblical concept of the family is heresy for statist philosophy, for it represents independence from state control. The trustee family must therefore be destroyed. The state welfare programme is one of the means used to destroy it. Thus for the statist the family is no more than a group of

---

3. R. J. Rushdoony, *The Institutes of Biblical Law* (Presbyterian and Reformed Publishing Company), p. 417.

4. *Ibid.*, p. 418.

genetically related individuals who share the same housing unit. They find their true meaning and function in life in terms of the state.

The biblical teaching on society and family is neither individualistic nor centralist, but emphasises man's responsibilities and privileges as a covenant creature in every area of life. The state as well as the family is thus a covenant institution which functions in terms of God's law-order—that is to say a Theocratically governed institution. Both state and family are important institutions in biblical society, but their respective roles are clearly separated. The function of the state is as a ministry of justice, a *civil* government limited to the administration of those laws with a civil duty or penalty attached to them. This is an area where biblical law maintains a clear institutional differentiation which has been blurred in our own times. It is not the prerogative of the state or civil magistrate to act as a ministry of welfare, economy or education, or in any other way interfere with the responsibilities of the family, except in the legitimate administration of those laws which it exists to uphold—which are considerably limited in God's word. Under the covenant that God has established with mankind the trustee family is responsible for the provision of these social needs.

The education, welfare, and stewardship of the economic resources of society are of central importance to the preservation and development of a civilisation. The fact that these areas of responsibility have been given specifically to the family in the Bible is significant. It meant that the family was the fundamental social unit in the covenant structure of the nation. The prosperity and future of the nation was thus entrusted primarily to the *family*, not to the state. It was from the heads of families that the officers of the national political and judicial structures were elected—e.g. elders, that is heads of households, clans and tribes, functioned as the civil, political and in the earlier period military leaders. The function of the family as trustee was therefore vital to the life of the whole community and had a significance which extended far beyond its own boundaries, in that the quality of family life and its faithfulness to the covenant would be reflected in the quality and character of the men who led the nation. The future of the nation thus depended upon the family's faithful discharge of its covenant responsibilities.[5]

Clearly, therefore, in the Bible the education of children is seen as a family responsibility. Children were to be educated within the context of the covenant life of the family under the authority and guardianship of its head (cf. Ps. 78:4-7).[6] The nature of the education provided was also to be covenantally structured; that is to say the father was responsible for ensuring that his children received an education which was God-centred and thus which enabled the child to understand his calling and duty in life as God's servant and image bearer. In other words the covenantal perspective was to govern the whole of the child's education (Ps. 78:4-7). Abraham is commended specifically because of his faithfulness in providing a godly

---

5. I am not arguing here for a patriarchal government of society—at least not in the sense that this term is usually used. In the Bible the authority of the family does not reign supreme. The family is one of three major institutions—the church and the state being the other two. Its authority, like that of church and state, is limited in Scripture and it should not cross the legitimate sphere of authority of either of these other two institutions, any more than they should cross that of the family. I am not arguing, therefore, that the *authority* of the family should extend beyond its institutional boundaries but simply that its *influence* inevitably does, the reason being that it is the foundational institution in society, to whose authority God has committed the essential tasks of welfare, economy (in the widest sense) and education, and therefore has a formative role to play in the development of the intellectual and moral character of its members, and thus of society as a whole.

6. It is true that one tribe, Levi, was appointed as the priestly tribe and given the special responsibility of teaching the law of God to the nation. But the Levites were not responsible for the general education of children. Rather, they were responsible for the religious education (in the narrower sense) of the nation. They were analogous to the teaching elders who labour in the word and in doctrine in the Christian era (1 Tim. 5:17).

education for his children and those born in his household (Gen. 18:19) in contrast to Lot, who, while maintaining his own personal piety, had evidently neglected, in the midst of an evil generation, to educate his children faithfully in terms of the requirements of the covenant (Gen. 19:14, 31-36).

Nor was it, moreover, to be simply a "religious education" in the narrowly defined sense of the term. History, jurisprudence, philosophy, ethics, economics, psychology, science etc. are all modern terms, but the substance of the disciplines they represent were all present in varying degrees in the Hebrew culture of biblical times—though instruction is given in the form of practical wisdom rather than abstract academic dissertations. The writer of The Book of Wisdom tells us that he had been given "true understanding of things as they are: a knowledge of the structure of the world and the operation of the elements; the beginning and end of epochs and their middle course; the alternating solstices and changing seasons; the cycles of the years and the constellations; the nature of living creatures and behaviour of wild beasts; the violent force of winds and the thoughts of men; the varieties of plants and the virtues of roots. I learnt it all, hidden or manifest, for I was taught by her whose skill made all things, wisdom."[7]

It was also the responsibility of the father, in Hebrew culture, to provide his son with a trade or means of livelihood. A well known Rabbinic maxim states: "He who does not teach his son a craft, teaches him to steal."[8] The reasoning behind this was that without a trade to provide a legitimate means of living one would be tempted to resort to theft.

This principle is as relevant today as ever and the soundness of the reasoning behind it has been demonstrated all too well in our own society. Many today who have no trade or employment as a legitimate means of livelihood—or who have

7. The Book of Wisdom (or Wisdom of Solomon) 7: 17-22.

8. The Babylonian Talmud, Kiddushin 29*a*.

no access to employment in their trade through, for example, trade union labour restriction cartels—have resorted to a form of legalised theft as a means of support, viz. state welfare handouts financed by excessive taxation or so-called "wealth redistribution" programmes. The decapitalisation of society resulting from these tax-financed welfare programmes threatens to destroy the traditional—and fundamentally biblical—structure of Western society, in that it not only creates a vast section of the community which is economically—and, given time, psychologically—dependent on the paternalistic state, but also, through financial strangulation due to oppressive taxation rates, makes it increasingly difficult for the family to fulfil its God-ordained duty to provide for the education and well-being of its members. State welfare programmes, in which the family's means of providing for its own are confiscated in order to support those on state welfare, is a form of theft and a major factor in the disintegration of the family as the basic social unit in society today. The modern state welfare programme thus constitutes a complete overturning of the system of family welfare, supplemented where necessary by the church and personal works of charity, which is set forth in Scripture.

New Testament teaching

When we turn specifically to the New Testament we find that this covenantal pattern of family responsibility remains unchanged. The New Testament makes it clear that the family is still the basic social unit with the same covenantal functions as trustee of its economic resources with responsibility for the education and welfare of its members (1 Tim. 5:4, 8, 16). The newness of the Christian covenant does not in any way abrogate the family's covenant responsibilities nor the basic family oriented nature of the covenant structure—not even with respect to the institutional church since elders, for instance, should be heads of households, family men who have proved that they are able to govern both themselves and their households in a godly way before they take on the government of the church (1 Tim. 3:2-13). God does not establish His covenant with men merely as individuals, but as they are the heads and representatives of their households (Gen. 17:7, 9, etc., Acts 11:14, 16:31).

This is not meant to imply that individuals cannot be in covenant with God or that salvation is simply a matter of being born into a Christian family irrespective of personal faith. But neither is salvation to be seen purely in individualistic terms. In other words the covenant relation established by God with man does not *terminate* in the individual; rather it *begins* with him and goes on to embrace those for whom he is covenantally responsible and whom he must represent before God. The family, including its adopted members, is party to the covenant since it is represented in its head.

This is so even from the soteriological perspective of the New Testament in which Jesus Christ is made manifest as the head and representative of the household of God (1 Cor. 11:3, Eph. 2:19, 5:23, Col. 1:18). It is through our *adoption* as sons of God that we share the blessings of covenant fellowship with God (Eph. 1:4-5). God dealt with Adam as the federal head of humanity, and with Jesus Christ, the last Adam, as the federal head of the new humanity. We are reconciled to God through adoption or incorporation into Christ (Gal. 3:26-29). He is the head to whom we hold and the source of our salvation. The prior soteriological importance of our membership in the household of God through the adoption in Jesus Christ does not, however, in any way invalidate or diminish the significance of the family as a covenantal unit. Both Old and New Testament believers are under the same covenant of grace in Jesus Christ and therefore the role and responsibilities of the family remain the same under both administrations. The family is the basic covenant institution, which exists within and itself helps to uphold the covenant structure of church, society and nation.

Thus, in the New Testament, as in the Old, the promise of salvation—that is to say of restoration into covenant fellowship with God—is made to the believer *and to his children* (Acts 2:39). Of course this promise is immediately qualified by the clause "as many as the Lord our God shall call to Himself." However, this qualification should not be taken as a virtual negation of the former promise, which indeed is implied if we presume that the children of believers are not to be accepted as Christians until they have some kind of conversion experience or are deemed to have "made their own decision to follow the Lord." And although it is through conversion experiences that many are brought to faith in Christ we must remember that a conversion experience is neither an essential element nor the biblical test of true faith. Certainly, such experiences should not be seen as the goal of a Christian education. Rather, the biblical norm is for our children to be *brought up* in the nurture and admonition of the Lord (Eph. 6:4). We are taught in Scripture to "train up a child in the way he should go, and when he is old he will not depart from it" (Pr. 22:6). It should be stated clearly that what is being said here is not meant to imply the doctrine of baptismal regeneration in any sense.[9] But it does mean that God will honour His covenant and be faithful to His promise. This promise, however, implies the shouldering of certain responsibilities on the part of those to whom it is made.[10] It is a *covenant* promise made to

---

9. These comments should not be taken primarily as a contribution to the debate between Baptists and paedo-baptists as to the validity of paedo-baptism. Unfortunately the lines are not so neatly and conveniently drawn. There are Baptists who do indeed bring up their children in the nurture and admonition of the Lord and thus provide them with an education which is covenantally faithful, and there are paedo-baptists who patently do not do so.

10. It needs to be stressed that this promise is made to Christian parents *as* parents. The idea that one can have faith for one's children, which has sometimes been advocated as an argument for paedo-baptism, is absurd and unbiblical. Clearly, one can only have faith on one's own account. Our faith

parents which requires covenant faithfulness on their part. We are to raise our children in the covenant as servants of God in fellowship with Him. It is a great encouragement to Christian parents, therefore, to know that God's hand is on their children and that they are to be treated as heirs of the kingdom of God unless and until, by their own profession or apostate behaviour, they show themselves to be otherwise.

Since the promise of salvation is to the believer *and* to his children it is the duty of believers to educate their children *in the Lord*, that is to say bring them up as *Christians*, not as pagans who must one day make an autonomous decision about their eternal destiny. Unfortunately the latter is too often the way that the children of believers are educated today. Yet it is a teaching of Scripture that the children of believers are to be accepted as members of the covenant community and brought up in the knowledge and fear of the Lord (1 Cor. 7:14), which means, among other things, providing them with an education which is God-centred and God-honouring, and which therefore prepares them for a life of service to God.

It is important to understand here that Christian parents are responsible not only for providing their children with an education, but also for the *kind* of education their children receive. For the Christian the purpose of education is to facilitate maturation in the image of God and thus growth into true manhood and true womanhood, so that the child might

---

cannot save another. But the promise is made to parents who are members of the covenant in Christ. Their covenant faithfulness clearly has implications for the children they represent before God, not because they can have faith on their children's behalf, but because they are acting in faith and obedience to a promise made to *themselves* as covenant members in the role of parents. In other words the promise of salvation for our children is made to *Christian parents* in their role *as* parents. The text says "the promise is to you and to *your* children." It is thus a promise made to *Christian parents* which is to be received and acted upon in faith *by* Christian parents; and this is why it is the duty of Christian parents to baptise their children in the faith and bring them up accordingly.

be able to fulfil his creation mandate in obedience to God's word. It follows from this that the kind of education we give our children must be one which is thoroughly grounded in the Christian world-view and which seeks to subject every discipline to the authority of God's word as it is revealed in the scriptures of the Old and New Testaments. Education is thus inescapably a covenant activity; indeed, it is a central aspect of man's covenant duty. Hence to deny our children such an education is to abandon our responsibilities as the covenant people of God.

The primary aim of education

It has been stated above that the purpose of education is to enable the child to mature in the image of God and thus equip him to fulfil his vocation in life as God's vicegerent and extend his dominion over the earth. If the child is to realise this calling he must attain *wisdom.* It is wisdom which in the Bible is set forth as the primary aim of education: "Acquire wisdom! Acquire understanding! . . . Do not forsake her and she will guard you; love her and she will watch over you. Wisdom is the primary thing; therefore get wisdom: and with all your acquiring get understanding" (Pr. 4:5-7).

Wisdom is more than either learning in the academic sense or "practical knowledge" in the popular sense. Nor is it mere intuition; it is *understanding* in the fullest sense of the word and thus something which is learned (Ps. 34:11). The wisdom literature is certainly educational literature, as indeed is the whole of Scripture; but the pursuit of wisdom is more than the modern secular idea of education. Wisdom is in a sense more than the sum of its parts, at least from the point of view of formal content. It includes, or rather is characterised by, an orientation in life, viz. a sense of service and duty to God, and above all a consciousness of the fact that life is lived in the presence of God and as a means of glorifying Him. Wisdom therefore comes ultimately from God (James 1:5) and is acquired in the submission of our lives and of our *minds* to His word in every discipline and field of study and in every walk of life. Thus "the fear of the Lord is the beginning of wisdom: and knowledge of the holy is understanding" (Pr. 9: 10).

Yet at the same time wisdom is not pietistic. It is intensely practical. The wisdom literature in the Bible is full of sound godly advice about living—and how little there is of that in many schools today! Indeed, much of modern educational philosophy is little more than studied stupidity and sheer folly.

J. E. Adams' comments on the nature and meaning of the biblical concept of wisdom are relevant here and worth quoting at length: "The principle Hebrew word for wisdom, *chokmah*, which permeates the thought of Old Testament *and* New Testament writers and has given rise to a genre of writing we call 'wisdom literature,' denotes *wisdom by experience*, not just by study. It also includes the idea of discrimination between good and evil, the receiving of instruction, attitude (or mind set), and the exercising of correct judgment and skills. The scope of the word is large, encompassing the totality of one's intellectual, living and performing experience. We have no equivalent term in English. Our own word, 'wisdom,' by contrast, is impoverished. It is a word that, in fact, rapidly seems to be disappearing from our vocabulary. Fundamentally, the biblical word *wisdom* brings together three factors: knowledge, life and ministry. It is knowledge, understanding from God's perspective, made profitable for day-to-day living for Him, and (as a part of that) shared with others and used to minister to them."[11]

The biblical philosophy of education, therefore, embraces more than the mechanics of acquiring knowledge or technical information. It aims at far more than the child's "self-fulfil-

11. Jay E. Adams, *Back to the Blackboard: Design for a Biblical Christian School* (Phillipsburg, New Jersey: Presbyterian and Reformed Publishing Company), p. 87f.

ment." Nor is it concerned merely with enabling the child to "play a useful part in society." It is concerned with the attainment of *wisdom*, and this involves an attitude or orientation in life of submission to the word of God and commitment to the truth revealed therein. Its purpose is to enable the child to fulfil his true calling to live in covenant fellowship with God and thus "to glorify God and to enjoy Him forever."

The place of the school

The absence of schools for the education of children in biblical society should not be taken to imply that schools as such are wrong or inconsistent with the philosophy of education set forth in Scripture.

It is true that the school is in no sense a biblical institution, that is to say it is not a God-ordained institution with a scripturally defined role to play in the covenant structure of the nation.[12] The God-ordained institution responsible for education is the family. Thus the school is not to be seen as a separate institution in life with its own sphere of authority in matters relating to education. Rather, the school offers a service to the family in the pursuit of its educational responsibilities. As a service for specialist training in specific subjects the school is a valid facility available for parents to make use of. But in making use of the service offered by the school Christian parents must ensure that its educational philosophy and practice are consistent with and will support and encourage the Christian covenantal perspective which should govern the child's education at every level.

---

12. Cf. J. E. Adams, *op. cit.*, p. 77ff. Elementary schools were established in Jewish culture in the early post-biblical period. Up until about the end of the second century A. D. they were usually private establishments. After that they became closely associated with the synagogue. On the development of early Jewish elementary education see Nathan Morris, *The Jewish School, An Introduction to the History of Jewish Education* (London: Eyre and Spottiswood, 1937).

However, the modern idea that education as such is the responsibility of the school—and in the wider sense of the school as the agent of the paternalistic state—and an area of the child's life which is set apart from the covenant life of the family under the authority and leadership of its head, is certainly inconsistent with the biblical philosophy of education. Institutional differentiation in which the responsibility and authority for the child's education is transferred from the God-ordained institution of the family to the school as an organ of the state is the product of humanism and an attempt by man to establish his independence from God and His covenant pattern for man's life. It is a form of social revolution against the covenant model set forth in God's word, and as such to be resisted fiercely by Christians and denounced publically by the church.

The private school, as an ancillary tool for parents to make use of in the education of their children, provides a valid service in society today; but again, it should not be seen as an institution in favour of which parents may abdicate their educational responsibilities.

Obviously, since Erasmus was the last person to know everything there was to know in his time it is not possible for parents today to specialise in all the fields of study which they may wish to offer to their children. Thus the school is a far more necessary service today than it was in biblical times. The extent of the knowledge available to the Hebrew people in biblical times was far more limited than that available to us today. It was possible for a father to educate his children in at least the basics of most subjects, and probably beyond to a degree not possible today.[13] Thus schools and freelance teach-

13. Many scholars seem to assume that the ordinary people in biblical society were illiterate (cf. Morris, *op. cit.*, p. 20-21 & 45). This is a hasty conclusion, however, too much based on perceptions of what was likely in terms of modern sociological models. On the contrary, it is evident from texts such as Deut. 6:8-9, 11:20, Is. 8:1, 10:19 that literacy was more wide-

ers with specialist skills—such as peripatetic musical instrumentalists—and other ancillary tools to facilitate learning in areas outside of the competence of parents, e.g. correspondence courses, are to be employed as much as necessary. This becomes more important in the higher levels of study. But in so using these facilities parents are not at liberty to turn over the formation of their children's world-view to institutions or individuals who are pagan and anti-covenantal in their outlook.

Conclusion

Parents are responsible for the *kind* of world-view their children imbibe, and for the *kind* of instruction they receive in specific subjects. Overall educational aims and perspective as well as the specific disciplines taught fall within the area of parental responsibility. Thus, teachers are said to be *in loco parentis*, that is to say taking the place of parents in the education of their children. It is therefore the responsibility of par-

---

spread than many modern scholars are prepared to accept. According to A. R. S. Kennedy, "It is now impossible to form an exact estimate of the extent to which education, as tested by the ability to read and write, was common among the people. The standard of learning would naturally be higher in the cities than in the country districts, highest of all in the neighbourhood of the court. Yet such facts as that Amos and Micah among the literary prophets belonged to the ranks of the people; that Mesha, king of Moab, could count on readers for the stele commemorating his victories; that the workmen who excavated the tunnel from the Virgin's spring to the pool of Siloam carved in the rock the manner of their work,—these facts, taken along with more than one passage in Isaiah (8:1, 10:19 'a child may write them'; cf. 29:11-12 the distinction between the literate and the illiterate), should make us pause before drawing the line of illiteracy too high in the social scale." ("Education" in James Hastings, ed., *A Dictionary of the Bible* [Edinburgh: T. & T. Clark], vol. I, p. 647*a*) It is not unreasonable to suspect, therefore, that the unwillingness of some to accept a more widespread level of literacy among the Hebrews of this period has more to do with a prior commitment to the idea of evolution than it has to a thorough investigation of the proper sources on which to base one's conclusions—viz. the biblical and archaeological records.

ents to ensure that their children are educated in terms of the Christian faith, not the religion of humanism and the Moloch state. God will require it of us.

4

EDUCATION AND DOMINION

As we have seen, education is a central aspect of the Christian's parental responsibilities under the covenant that God has established with His people. In order to appreciate the significance of the role that education occupies in the outworking of this covenant we need to understand the biblical teaching on the covenant. We have already looked briefly at the nature of the covenant.[1] We shall now consider the purpose and scope of the covenant and the bearing this has on education. The significance of the role that education plays in the covenant life of God's people will become apparent when it is seen in this broader context, and the necessity of a specifically Christian philosophy and practice of education even more so, since it is this broader context which gives education its proper direction, that is to say its purpose and vision in practical terms.

The creation mandate

The purpose of the covenant relation that God has established with mankind is to enable man to serve and glorify God by fulfilling his cultural mandate as God's vicegerent on earth. This cultural mandate is clearly set forth in Genesis: "God created man in His own image . . . male and female He cre-

1. See above p. 52ff.

ated them. And God blessed them and said to them, 'Be fruitful and multiply, and replenish the earth, and subdue it; and have dominion over the fish of the sea, and over the fowl of the air, and over every living thing that moves on the earth'" (Gen. 1:27-28). This is man's cultural or creation mandate, his calling in terms of the purpose of God, and it is a necessary consequence of the fact that man is created in God's image. Hence the Westminster Shorter Catechism rightly ties together inseparably these two aspects of man's nature: "God created man male and female, after his own image, in knowledge, righteousness, and holiness, with dominion over the creatures" (Q. 10, *A.*).

Indeed, the cultural mandate is an aspect of the image of God in man. Since God is the sovereign ruler of His creation, having absolute authority and total dominion, man, who is created in His image, is to reflect in a creaturely way that dominion and rulership through his stewardship of the earth under the guidance of God's law. That is to say, just as the image of God in man consists of knowledge, righteousness and holiness because God is an omniscient, righteous and holy God, so also it properly involves dominion over the creatures since God is the sovereign Lord of creation in whose image man has been created and thus whose communicable attributes, including that of dominion, he is to reflect as he images God on earth. In other words, since man is created in God's image he thinks God's thoughts and does God's works after Him, not in an original creative way, but in a re-creative imitative way. Hence the creation mandate given in Genesis 1:28 stipulates that man should take dominion over the earth and subdue it for the glory of God and his own benefit, just as God, in a much higher sense as the sovereign Lord of creation, rules over His creation and works all things for His own glory.

Hence also the apostle Paul in Ephesians chapter five instructs us to be "imitators of God" (v. 1). A little further on (v.

22ff.) he shows us what this means, how it is worked out in practical terms, in our family life. We are told to act in a certain way and to do certain things because this is how God has acted and what God has done for us. We are told that the husband is to be the head of the wife, just as Christ is the head of the church. Therefore just as the church is subject to Christ so also the wife should be subject to her husband. Likewise, husbands are to love their wives just as Christ loved the church and gave himself up for it (vv. 23-25). In the same way a father must discipline and chasten his children just as God disciplines and chastens his people; and this must be done in the context of loving care just as God disciplines his people out of loving care for them. And without this there can be no dominion in our family life, as our age sadly demonstrates all too well. Without this loving discipline and chastening children will not learn to govern themselves under the covenant according to God's law and thus they will not be able to take godly dominion over the earth.

Dominion in our domestic life, therefore, is achieved by imaging or imitating God in the way we relate to each other as members of a family. Likewise, in every other area of life and thought we are to image God on earth by thinking God's thoughts and doing God's works after Him. Imaging God in a creaturely way is how man takes dominion as God's vicegerent and thus fulfills his cultural mandate; and God has clearly made known to man *how* he is to do this in His law-word.

This dominion is, as R. J. Rushdoony has written, "*first* of all over ourselves, *second*, with respect to our calling, and, *third*, over the natural realm, the world around us, biologically, agriculturally, commercially, historically, and so on."[2] As Rushdoony rightly points out, this dominion "is not domination; it is the exercise of godly authority, power, and oversight wher-

---

2. R. J. Rushdoony, "Calvinism and Culture" in *Calvinism Today*, vol. I, no. 1 (January, 1991), p. 4*a*.

ever God gives us the responsibility."[3] The extent of this creation mandate is clearly set forth in Genesis 1:28: man is to subdue the whole earth and rule over every living creature that moves upon the face of the earth. Man's dominion is to be world-wide and all embracing. He is the steward of God's creation and therefore responsible to God for the productive exploitation and management of the earth and its resources. Hence man's calling is to godly dominion over the whole earth and in every area of his life, thought and work. He is to develop both his own potential and that of the world he has been given to rule over as the means by which he is to serve and glorify his Creator.

The covenant regulates and governs *how* man is to take dominion over the earth in the fulfilling of this creation mandate. Man's calling to subdue the earth and exercise dominion over it is embraced totally by the covenant, and it is in terms of the requirements of that covenant, that is to say in terms of the covenant law, that he is to realise this calling. Thus the covenant, as we have already seen, is the supreme and all-embracing fact of life for man. Man cannot escape its requirements, nor his responsibilities under it. As a covenant keeper man lives in fellowship with God and receives the blessings and privileges of adoption into the household of God in Christ. As a covenant breaker he stands under the curse of the covenant law and the sentence of eternal death it pronounces against all who transgress its commandments. In either case the sanctions of the covenant are inescapable for man, since man is in all things, by virtue of his creation in the image of God, a covenant creature and required by God to think and act in conformity with and obedience to the all-embracing covenant that God has established as the basic principle of human existence.

---

3. *Ibid.*

Fall and redemption

When Adam sinned he rejected the definitive interpretation of reality set forth by God's word and attempted to frame his own definition and interpretation of the world he was in, to determine for himself how he should live and impose his own concept of order and law onto reality. He would thus make himself the ultimate judge and his own ideas the ultimate authority in all predication. This was Adam's original sin, and it is this sin which constitutes the foundation of all sins. It is this condition of rejecting God and His authority into which all men are born by nature since the fall.

In this condition of rebellion man attempts to rid himself and the world around him of God and His word as the basis of all understanding by rejecting God and His creative purpose as the fundamental principle of interpretation of reality in every aspect of its being. Man attempts to deprive the created order of God and His purpose, and as a result he becomes totally depraved, since he refuses to acknowledge God in all things. In every aspect of his being he denies God and His will and seeks instead a life of autonomy. This is the meaning of the doctrine of total depravity: it is not that man is incapable of doing anything that is in itself good, for he is evidently capable of that, but that in all he is and does in this fallen unredeemed state, good or bad, he denies God and His purpose. Thus man denies God and His dominion in the totality of life and lives instead under the dominion of sin. Only on his own terms will man allow God back into the scheme of things as determined by his own autonomous rationality; that is to say only a God who is basically a construct of man's own rationality, a God made in the image of man, is deemed to be acceptable or reasonable. Thus man frames his own religion with his own god, a "religion within the limits of pure reason" as man sees it. This rebellion against God's authority thus aims to overturn the order of creation as God intended it. It is a radical defacing of reality by man, an attempt to overthrow the One who alone can give meaning to the world in which man lives, and therefore its end is the death of man and of his culture.

It is only through God's saving grace in Jesus Christ that man is delivered from this condition and restored to his original position as God's legitimate vicegerent over the earth. Outside of Christ man is under the dominion of sin. In Christ man is delivered from that dominion into the dominion of grace and of God's kingdom, and his original dominion mandate is restored. However, a far greater blessing awaits mankind in Christ than was his before the fall. In Christ God's people are predestined to the adoption as sons in the household of God. Their perseverance is sure and they live as kings and priests of God in Christ, their new covenant head.

Thus in Christ man's dominion mandate is renewed and expanded to account for God's redemptive purpose. Man's calling as God's vicegerent over the earth is restored, since the covenant relation between God and man is renewed and its *substance* ratified in Christ. But the *form* of the covenant is new. Man is restored to communion with God by *grace* through *faith*, and thus it is a covenant of redemptive grace in Jesus Christ. This means that man's original creation mandate is now enlarged to take account of the Great Commission given by Christ to His church to preach the gospel and make disciples of all nations (Matt. 28:18-20). Thus the Christian mandate incorporates the creation mandate and the Great Commission. The people of God are to bring the gospel of Christ to bear upon all things and subject every thought and deed to the authority and rule of Jesus Christ (2 Cor. 10:4-5).

The covenant[4]

The covenant relation to which man is restored by faith in Christ is thus a covenant of *dominion* in Jesus Christ. The work of Christ has brought about a renewing of all things. Of course this renewing of all things finds its ultimate consummation in eternity; nevertheless, the historical fact of Christ's incarnation, death, resurrection and ascension means that this work of renewal has already begun in history and will progress through time towards its consummation at the end of the age. Calvary, therefore, is the focal point of all history, the event upon which the history of men and nations, and indeed of the whole world, turns. Through Christ man is redeemed and restored in his calling as God's vicegerent on earth. In Christ he is once again a prophet, priest and king, proclaiming the good news of redemption through Christ and bringing all things into subjection to Christ. His task is to bring Christ's rule into every area and aspect of life. The Great Commission is thus the renewal of man's original creation mandate, but taking account of man's fall into sin and his redemption through faith in Jesus Christ. It is the creation mandate plus the proclamation of man's deliverance from the dominion of sin and his restoration into covenant fellowship with God in Christ.

God's law sets forth the terms of this covenant with its promises and blessings on God's part and its obligations on man's part, as well as its cursings and judgements against those who transgress its commands. Those who through faith look to Jesus Christ alone for salvation are delivered from these judgements of the law against sin, since Christ bore the curse of the law in their place, as it is written: "Christ redeemed us from the curse of the law, having become a curse for us" (Gal. 3:13). Those who put their faith in Christ are thus delivered from the law as an indictment against sin. They are no longer under law—i.e. under the sentence of the law—but under grace. In regeneration the believer has God's law written on his heart by the indwelling work of the Holy Spirit so that he

4. See Appendix A for a more detailed statement of the nature of the covenant.

obeys God's commandments willingly out of love for God, and not out of fear of judgement.

Thus man is restored to covenant fellowship with God by means of God's free grace through faith in Christ. As a believer he is not under a covenant of works as a means of justification; but he is by grace through faith delivered from sin—which is the transgression of the law—and renewed in the inner man so that he delights to serve God and obey His law. The law remains for the believer a perfect definition of righteousness and thus the standard by which he is sanctified in Christ's image—for Christ kept the law perfectly. The law, therefore, remains a constant factor in the covenant of grace and thus in the life of the believer also, but the believer's *relationship* to the law is changed under the covenant of grace (Rom. 7:1-4). He is no longer under the law as a sentence of death, since Christ has borne that death sentence for him. But he is under the law as a way of life, a rule of conduct, that is to say as a way of living righteously and of fulfilling his calling to subdue the earth and exercise dominion over it; and through the indwelling Spirit he is renewed and given grace and help to obey God's law (Rom. 8:4). The covenant of grace is thus the restoration of man into covenant fellowship with God by means of grace through faith in Christ.

This covenant under which man is redeemed in Jesus Christ embraces the whole of man's life, just as the original covenant with Adam embraced the whole of life. To limit the scope of this covenant is to limit the nature of the redemption that Christ purchased for His elect. Christ died to redeem the *whole* man, that is to say His death was a price paid for the redemption of the whole man, and thus every area and aspect of his life, not just the "soul." Christ's redeeming work embraces the whole man in the whole course of his life. It affects his inward and his outward life, his private life and his culture.

The Christian covenant, therefore, comprehends and *governs* the whole of man's life. It embraces not only his private, vocational and family life (areas of personal responsibility), but church and state also (areas of public responsibility). Since Christ died to redeem the whole man in the whole course of his life, these areas of public responsibility come under the *rule* of Jesus Christ and are aspects of our covenant life in Him. The Christian covenant is all embracing; it covers the personal and vocational life of man, and also the spheres of family, church and state. The covenant relation to which man is restored in Christ finds its proper expression in the faithful exercise of the creation mandate and the Great Commission in obedience to God's law, confirmed by Christ in Matt. 5:17 and 28:18-20. Both the creation mandate and the Great Commission are necessary to man's calling as God's vicegerent on earth, for only when both are given their full significance will the Christian community truly represent Christ's body on earth, reigning as kings through the exercise of godly dominion in obedience to their creation mandate, ministering as prophets of Christ by proclaiming His word to a fallen world, and exercising their priestly calling to bring all things into subjection to Jesus Christ in obedience to the Great Commission.[5] The covenant that God has established with his people is thus a covenant of redemptive grace *and* dominion in Jesus Christ.[6]

The role of education

As we have already seen, the family has a vitally important role to play in society through its educational responsibilities. It is in the context of family life that the child learns to govern

5. On man's role as prophet, priest and king see R. J. Rushdoony, *Salvation and Godly Rule* (Vallecito: Ross House Books, 1983), p. 437 ff.

6. As proof of this we need only consider that God has given the nations and the ends of the earth to His Son as His inheritance, that He rules them with a rod of iron (Ps 2:8-9), and that the children of God by adoption into the household of God through faith in Christ are joint-heirs with Christ and share His inheritance and dominion over the earth (Rom. 8:16-17, Eph. 1:5, Matt. 5:5).

himself through the discipline and education he receives from his parents and those to whom they may delegate their authority in schools etc. As he learns and grows in this way he is equipped for responsibility in his future calling, in his family life as a parent himself, and also for responsibility in church and state should he be called thereto.

It is in terms of his understanding of the scope of the covenant that education finds its significance for the Christian. Education is the means by which the child is trained for life in his God-given role as vicegerent over the earth, governing all things under his authority according to God's word, proclaiming the sovereign word of God in all things, and bringing all things into subjection to Christ. If the child is to be equipped to fulfil this calling it is important that a Christian philosophy and practice of education should be pursued at every level in the child's development and in every subject within the curriculum, academic or otherwise.

In every subject and in all areas of life, and at all ages, in church, at home, at school, at work etc., we are, as Christians, growing up and learning our duty to God in Christ. This is so for all Christians at all times. It is important, however, that the child should be nurtured in such a life of service from the very beginning. We are commanded to "put on the Lord Jesus Christ and make no provision for the flesh" (Rom. 13:14 cf. Gal. 3:27, Eph. 4:24). This does not mean merely that we should abstain from obvious sexual sins etc., but that the whole course of our lives is to be characterised by conformity to the image of God in Christ, and that we are to make no provision for the denial of God and His word in our lives.

This has important and far-reaching implications for the kind of education we provide for our children. An education that denies God and His word as the interpretive principle of all things, including all academic disciplines, is an education that implicitly denies the whole of biblical truth and the validity of Christian faith. To subject our children to such an education is to deny the sovereignty and Lordship of God over our children and thus apostasy from the faith. As Christians we are to subject all things to the rule of Christ and the authority of His word, and we are to *understand* all things in terms of His word, whether in the fields of theology, morality, history, art, commerce, archaeology, cosmology, philosophy or whatever area of life we seek to understand and develop. For parents this means that at every level and in every area of the child's growth and development, both morally *and* academically, he is to be nurtured in the word of God and instructed in terms of a Christian world-view which brings all aspects of his education under the definitive interpretation of reality set forth in God's word. All subjects, therefore, must be brought into conformity with God's revelation and taught on the basis of the Christian world-view set forth in that revelation.

Without such an education the child will not mature in his calling to image God as His vicegerent over the earth, for education is the training ground for that task. The child must be trained in self-government under God in his personal, vocational and family life—and it is only as he learns to govern himself and his family in this way that he is equipped and thus permitted by God's word to bear office in church and state, should he be called to that task. His education, therefore, must be *dominion* oriented at all points, that is to say it must prepare him to exercise godly authority, power and oversight wherever he is given responsibility. The purpose of Christian education is to equip man for dominion in Christ through the whole course of his life, for his vicegerency on earth is an aspect of his creation in the image of God.

The meaning of discipline

Christian discipline must be aimed at achieving this God-given dominion task. It must be dominion oriented discipline, that is a regime of self-government under God in accordance with God's creative purpose for man. It is important here that we do not confuse discipline with punishment. The two are not the same, though both are essential for the child's development and growth in Christ. Punishment is what happens, or should happen, when discipline breaks down. Discipline, according to *The Oxford Concise Dictionary*, is "behaviour according to established rules." Godly discipline, or Christian discipline, is behaviour according to God's established rules as laid down in His law. Furthermore, the word *discipline* comes from the Latin word for disciple, *discipulus*, which is itself derived from the verb *disco*, meaning *to learn*. Thus, as R. J. Rushdoony has pointed out, "To be a disciple and to be under discipline is to be a learner in a learning process. If there is no learning, and no growth in learning, there is no discipline."[7]

It should be obvious, therefore, that godly discipline is impossible without godly *learning*. No amount of mere punishment can produce Christian discipline on its own. Without godly learning punishment produces nothing. It is only against the background of a loving environment in which the child is learning to think and act obediently in all things that punishment has value and meaning.

As Christian parents we are commanded to train up our children in the nurture and admonition of the Lord, that is to train them in godly discipline by means of godly *learning*. How can this be done if our children receive ungodly learning in state and pagan public schools? Ungodly learning produces discipline in terms of ungodly principles. To subject our children to ungodly learning is to subject them to ungodly discipline, and thereby to train them up to be pagans under a pagan discipline. Such an education is a total reversal of the biblical pattern of education, and apostasy from the faith far

7. R. J. Rushdoony, *The Institutes of Biblical Law* (Presbyterian and Reformed Publishing Company, 1973), p. 766.

more serious than the trifling departures from established church tradition that so many who send their children to state schools are continually at pains to expose in their brethren. Such nitpicking and judging of others can be observed in churches the length and breadth of the country each Sunday, especially among Reformed and evangelical churches. It is truly amazing how Christians can sit in church and criticise their brethren for failing to observe man-made traditions and rules that are of minor importance to say the least, and even feverishly guard their pulpits and communion tables from those who do not adhere to their particular confessional standards, and yet they will send their children to state schools to receive ungodly learning and ungodly discipline without batting an eyelid. Such ungodly behaviour is not according to Christian discipline, God's established rules of behaviour for parents; it is pharisaism of the worst kind, for those who engage in it not only vitiate their own witness but bring ruin upon the next generation by failing to provide an education for their children in terms of godly learning. Those who thus subject their children to ungodly learning in this way should consider the words of Christ: "Permit the children to come unto me, and stop hindering them" (Luke 18:16).

To subject our children to ungodly learning is to subject them to ungodly discipline and to hinder them from coming to Christ. It is thus a denial of the covenant that God has established with His people. The Bible condemns this. It is our duty—and it should be our *pleasure*—to raise our children in the learning and discipline of the Christian faith, and that means providing a godly education, learning in terms of godly principles, in every sphere of life and at every level. It also means educating the child for dominion under the covenant that God has made with His people. The child must learn to take his place in the adult world as God's vicegerent and therefore he must be trained to exploit it according to God's law for his own benefit and for the benefit of mankind, for by so doing he glorifies his Creator whose purpose he serves thereby. The Christian's calling is one of dominion in Christ, not escape from the world, and therefore the aim of a Christian education should be to train up the child into that dominion.

The Christian must overcome the world (1 John 5:4), and this can only be achieved by godly learning and godly discipline in all things, and by obedience to God's established rules of behaviour. Of course this is only possible through the influence of the Holy Spirit in our lives. But this is *how* He works in enabling God's people to overcome the world. Likewise, in the education of our children, godly learning combined with behaviour according to God's established rules of conduct, His law, must characterise the whole educational enterprise.

Conclusion

Education is a covenant responsibility for Christian parents, that is to say it finds its proper context and meaning in terms of the covenant that God has established with His people and under which they are redeemed by Christ from the dominion of sin in order that they might live a life of service to God in all things. The education of our children, therefore, must be pursued in conformity with the nature and conditions of that covenant at all points. As we have seen, this covenant is a covenant of redemptive grace *and* dominion in Jesus Christ, and thus we must educate our children for *dominion* in Christ as members of His covenant people.

5

NAMING THE ANIMALS: A CASE STUDY IN GODLY LEARNING

Understanding the world around us is essential for our dominion over it. But our understanding must be according to truth. We can only take dominion over the earth properly, i.e. according to God's will, as we come to understand the proper nature and function of the various aspects and elements of the world around us according to the creative purpose of the One who brought that world into being in the first place.

This is the meaning of Adam's naming of the animals in Genesis 2:19-20. The Lord God brought the animals to Adam so that he might name them and thereby take dominion over them. Very clearly, this was a process of *learning*, of education in the fullest sense, leading to greater dominion over the animals. This story, therefore, represents a perspicuous example of the place of education and learning according to godly principles in man's calling as God's image bearer and vicegerent on earth.

There are a number of important points to be considered in this account: *first*, to name something in biblical times meant more than it does in twentieth century Western culture today. It meant far more than merely assigning an arbitrary label to something, and therefore it is easy to miss the significance of the task given to Adam for our understanding of the educational enterprise. To name something in Scripture means to *describe* it, to *define the meaning* of something. A name in Scripture means something therefore. Thus, Abraham means *father of a multitude* (from the Hebrew *'ab*, father, and *rabah*, which is Arabic for multitude), a name that surely required great faith on the part of Abraham since he had no children when he was given this name by God.

Thus, in order for Adam to name the animals he had to understand them and their place in the created order of things first. Naming means describing, defining, and therefore necessitates understanding. Adam was given the task of understanding the animal kingdom, of learning about it, classifying the animals and giving appropriate descriptive names to the various species etc. This was a major zoological task requiring hard work and great ability in understanding.

Second, this is an account of man's pre-fall experience of learning and dominion, and is therefore instructive with regard to how man is to seek knowledge obediently. The way in which Adam undertook this task, the principles of interpretation he used to classify the data and determine its meaning and purpose, and most importantly the epistemological basis on which he worked, must be considered normative for obedient thinking and learning by the Christian today. Adam's naming of the animals, therefore, represents a true paradigm for human learning in all things.

Third, we are told that the *Lord God* created and brought the animals to Adam so that he might name them. The whole account takes place against the background of a God-created and God-interpreted universe ordered according to His purpose and under His government. The animals that Adam named, therefore, were not mere facts, unordered data floating around in an unordered universe which was meaningless until the mind of man imposed his own idea of order and meaning onto it. The data to which Adam applied his understanding and interpretive abilities was already defined and interpreted according to God's creative purpose. Adam's rational faculties were God-created faculties operating in a God-given and God-interpreted context. All the facts with which Adam dealt were already God-interpreted facts and Adam was engaged in a process of learning the truth about those facts by thinking God's thoughts after Him. He assumed, at this stage at least, the God-given and God-interpreted nature of the subject matter before him. He did not begin by assuming that the animal kingdom could be understood and interpreted independently of the God who created it and gave meaning to it. Rather, Adam understood, interpreted, classified and named the animals *as God brought them to him*, that is to say in terms of their God-given purpose. His learning, defining, categorising and naming were based on the God-given and God-interpreted nature of reality, and thus his understanding of the animals was based on their meaning in terms of God's creative purpose.

Not until the fall did Adam reject this God-given and God-interpreted nature of reality and of the data confronting him and choose instead to determine the nature and meaning of reality independently of God according to his own autonomous reason—a move which led to drastically incorrect conclusions about the trustworthiness of God's word and the nature of reality, resulting in the death of man as God had warned. Had Adam taken this step into autonomous human reasoning and denied the God-given nature of the data before him when he began the task of naming the animals he could not have understood and defined their true meaning and purpose in God's world and thus would have named them incorrectly. Adam's knowledge and learning at this point presupposed the God-created nature of reality and the fact that only as he thought God's thoughts after Him would his knowledge be according to truth and hence reliable.

Since Adam's naming of the animals is a paradigm for obedient learning, i.e. a normative model for the process of human learning in all things, this means that at the outset in all of our thinking, learning and teaching we must accept the definitive interpretation of reality set down in God's word as an authoritative and trustworthy guide to the meaning of reality and all things in it. Only to the extent that we do this shall we have a sound basis for our understanding of the data confronting us as we seek to interpret the world in which we live. The alternative is mere human speculation founded on nothing more substantial than human fantasy. Thus, all knowledge is based ultimately on *faith*, either in God and His definitive interpretation of reality set forth in His revelation, or else in man's capacity for creative speculation—viz. human fantasy.[1]

Obviously, knowledge sought in terms of a false understanding of reality, and a false interpretation of the data based on that view of reality—e.g. evolutionary myth—will lead us away from the truth as defined by God's creative purpose and into error, as it did with Adam over the issue of the fruit of the tree of the knowledge of good and evil, resulting in death for mankind and the subjection of the earth to God's curse (Gen. 3:14-19). Only as we approach a given subject with a commitment to the fundamental truth of the God-created and God-interpreted nature of reality as the bedrock of our thinking, as Adam did with the naming of the animals, shall our attempts to understand the world around us bear fruit.[2]

Fourth, the knowledge of the created order that Adam gained

---

1. I do not mean to deny or decry man's ability for creative thinking by any means. This is a very necessary aspect of his creation in the image of God. God is the Creator, and thus man also thinks and acts creatively as he images God on earth. But man's creative ability is not original; it is a communicable attribute of God and therefore man creates by imitating God. Life would be unthinkable for man without this creative ability, indeed it would cease to be human, for without the fruits of man's creativity his culture would be reduced to the level of that of the animals. What is denied here is that man's creative abilities are autonomous, original and hence definitive of reality, as pagan scientists and philosophers would have us believe (see the citations from Karl Popper and Immanuel Kant on p. 33f. Cf. the citation from H. Dooyeweerd in Chapter One, p. 15n.).

2. See Chapter One for a discussion of how the non-believer does this unwittingly by basing his knowledge on principles borrowed from an understanding of reality as God-created, and the results of this when it comes into conflict with the principle of the autonomy of human reason.

from this task was not mere theory, but led to greater maturity and wisdom which issued in a more fully developed understanding of his creation mandate and greater cultural progress. The are two aspects to this:

(1) By undertaking this work Adam learned not only about the nature of the animal kingdom, but also discovered something about his own nature and role in the world as God's image bearer which was vital to humanity, both physically and psychologically: "Adam gave names to all the cattle, and to the fowl of the air, and to every beast of the field; *but for Adam there was not found an help meet for him*" (Gen. 2:20). Mankind was made male and female in God's purpose. Through this task Adam discovered his need for companionship and thus Eve was created from Adam to be his wife and help. Furthermore, *procreation* is important for man's dominion over the earth, and this was so before the fall, and thus before death entered in. Indeed procreation is essential for the fulfilling of the creation mandate. The development of man's dominion over the earth, the exploitation of the earth's natural resources and cultural progress generally only become possible with the division of labour and the specialisation of knowledge and technology. This necessitates procreation: "Be fruitful and *multiply*, and *fill* the earth, and subdue it" (Gen. 1:28).

(2) The animal kingdom constitutes a valuable resource for mankind in innumerable ways, and Adam's greater knowledge of the animals enabled him to exploit this resource more rationally and productively for his own benefit and for the benefit of the animal kingdom itself, and all to the glory of God. The knowledge Adam gained from this task would enable him to train and utilise the animals more effectively in his calling to cultivate the earth. The development of animal husbandry, the breeding of species particularly useful to man, and the use of animals for furs and leather etc. were practical results of this task. The preservation of rare species and breeding of better stock were also results which were of benefit to

the animal kingdom itself (cf. Gen. 30:41-42). Thus, the naming of the animals enabled Adam to extend his dominion over the earth. This task was the beginning of the process of civilising the earth on the practical level.

The task of naming the animals, therefore, was clearly set in the context of Adam's dominion mandate; indeed it was an essential aspect of that mandate. It was an educational programme aimed at extending his mastery over the world he was given to rule over. This process of education, of learning and growth in the understanding of God's creation and man's part in it, is essential to man's stewardship of the earth and to his calling to have dominion over it. It is not something that stands on its own, an end in itself. It has a purpose. That purpose is to train man into his calling under God and is thus fulfilled only as he exercises that calling. Education is the means of preparing man for his God-given task of subduing and replenishing the earth as God's image bearer.

The context of the educational task for the Christian, therefore, is the covenant, which, as we have seen, is a covenant of redemptive grace and dominion in Jesus Christ. Education is the process of training man into his calling to exercise dominion over the earth under the covenant that God has established with His people. In order to exploit the earth properly and productively man must be trained into his role as a steward and manager of the earth's resources. That role involves understanding God's purpose for the creation, observing the limits and boundaries to man's actions in achieving that dominion, which are set down in God's law-word, and utilising the earth and its resources productively for the betterment of mankind and of the earth itself. This is the calling of man in terms of God's purpose for mankind and for the world in which he lives, and it is as he pursues this calling obediently that he works for God and for His glory, and thus worships his creator according to His word.[3]

Education is the training process by which man learns to

shoulder this calling, and therefore it is vitally important that in every subject and at every level this learning process should presuppose the God-created and God-interpreted nature of reality, and that it should be pursued in terms of godly principles of thought and action throughout.

This is why Adam's naming of the animals is so important and instructive for us. It was a process of learning geared to man's creation mandate to have dominion over the earth. Education cannot properly be separated from man's calling in terms of the purpose of God, since he will either be educated for dominion as God's vicegerent, or else for autonomy, and that means in the end the domination of man by man and the subjugation of men not to God and His purpose, but to men and their corrupt desires, and even to the creation itself. Education is the training programme for man's calling to have dominion over the earth, and that calling is the context of man's whole life. He will pursue that calling according to God's purpose as revealed in His word, or he will do one of two things: either he will abuse his powers and abilities and his lordship over the earth in order to grasp power and authority for himself disobediently, or he will surrender his calling as lord over the earth and subject himself to the elements of nature to be ruled by them instead of ruling over them. Either option means the enslaving of the mass of mankind to the created order. Both have a long history and are still with us—e.g. totalitarian tyranny, and the practice of pagan religions such as Hinduism.[4]

Thus, the provision of education for our children must take account of man's calling in the purpose of God if it is to be a godly education, a "training in righteousness; that the man of God may be adequate, equipped for every good work" (2 Tim. 3:16-17). That calling necessitates a proper under-

---

3. On the nature and meaning of worship in relation to man's dominion mandate see Appendix B.

4. See Chapter Six for a more detailed discussion of this.

standing of man and of the world in which he lives in terms of the purpose of God. Only in the context of that calling do the various aspects of the educational task find their proper meaning, and only as the content of the education we provide for our children takes account of that calling will it enable them to mature in terms of the image of God.

For the Christian, education is the means by which man is trained into his covenant task of dominion; it is a training in "godly authority, power and oversight wherever God gives us the responsibility,"[5] over ourselves, over our vocations, and over the natural realm. Education for the Christian, therefore, cannot be separated from the all-pervasive context of God's purpose for man under the covenant of redemptive grace and dominion in Jesus Christ. To pursue human autonomy, and to educate for human autonomy, is to pervert man's being and stunt his growth into a mature creature in terms of God's purpose. It is to pervert the nature and calling of man, who is made in the image of God to think God's thoughts after Him. It is thus a denial of humanity as created and defined in the image of God. It is no wonder, therefore, that in an age of rampant atheism and human autonomy taken to its extremes there is so much depression, alienation, suicide, abortion etc. In the humanist schools of our land children are constantly trained into the frustration and denial of their humanity as created by God, and the end is death, both for the individual and for his culture.

By contrast, the educational task undertaken by Adam in his naming of the animals was a process of godly learning that led to the greater fulfilment of his calling as God's vicegerent on earth and thus to greater maturity as a human being made in the image of God. Adam named the animals in terms of God's creative purpose, and this led to maturity in under-

5. R. J. Rushdoony, "Calvinism and Culture" in *Calvinism Today*, vol. I, no. 1 (January, 1991), p. 4*a*.

standing and to the extension of man's dominion over the earth to the glory of God.

6

EDUCATION AND CIVILISATION

To deny the covenantal nature of man's life and his dominion over the world is to dehumanise mankind. As God's vicegerent and thus lord over the earth man is above all other creatures. Unlike the animals man is made of the earth physically, but his spirit is from God, that is to say he is created in the image of God. That image consists in a moral nature created for fellowship with God and dominion over the earth. To deny this necessarily moral and dominical nature of man is to dehumanise him since it is to strip him of all that properly constitutes the image of God in man. Hence, in his futile—and of course impossible—attempt to escape from God and from the moral nature of his being, man resorts to all manner of degraded and perverse practices. He attempts to degrade himself to the level of the animals, though in so doing he goes one better and resorts to practices which are not to be found even among the animals.

The pagan revival

Quite logically, therefore, given its anti-theistic world-view, Satanism proclaims as its most fundamental doctrine, that man is no different from and thus no higher than the animals. At least this is what Satanism claims, and doubtless many believe. Our age has demonstrated the outworking of this principle in many ways and on many levels and by many diverse groups—by no means all or even most of which would or indeed could self-conciously acknowledge their commitment to the principles of Satanism. These range from the degraded and bestial practices of sexual perversion to the more philosophical and ideological stance of the Green and ecology movements, the neo-paganism of the New Age movement, and the Animal Rights people who have resorted to the anti-human tactics of terrorism in an attempt to make their point and enforce their ideology on society. All this is the natural outworking of fallen man's desire to rid himself of his Creator. Since man's life is inextricably covenantal, and therefore moral in nature—man being created in God's image—man attempts to defy and deny God by overturning the God-ordained and thus natural order of creation and by denying his own moral nature, and in doing so he necessarily defaces his own humanity.

This is no digression from the point at issue, viz. education, for we must not be unaware of the current ability of most of the above mentioned groups, including sexual perverts, and the Green, New Age and Animal Rights movements, as well as humanism in general, to impose their viewpoints through the educational establishment. Our society is experiencing a very real return to paganism, the consequences of which will be far-reaching in our own lives, but even more so for the lives of our children and grandchildren. We must not underestimate the strategic importance of the educational establishment in this re-paganisation of society. It is not simply that the schools, colleges and universities of our land are not immune to the influence of neo-paganism; they are essential to the transmission of a culture's world-view, and if the culture is to be captured by neo-paganism it is these institutions which must be in the vanguard. Capture the schools and colleges and you have control of the next generation through the formation of its religious outlook and philosophy of life.

It will hardly be denied that humanism has captured most of our educational institutions, whether state or private, secular or religious. But many may be unaware of the degree to which groups such as the Green movement, Animal Rights and New Age people—and even the homosexual lobby to some extent[1]—are attempting, and with no little success, to infiltrate and influence the educational institutions of our land. It has been pointed out by teachers within the state system that such groups are increasingly seeking to offer their "educational" services to schools by providing courses for children and training for staff in their particular perspective. These teachers represent probably the few who have recognised this influence for what it is and rejected it. Many more, far less aware of the issues involved, are doubtless taken in by these groups, or even embrace their perspective wholeheartedly. Such groups are able to exercise a subliminal influence on our culture through the "services" they offer to schools as well as through the ongoing teaching work of those committed to their perspective within the state system. Increasing representation of such views in the media helps to soften up society and leads to a general growth in their acceptance, and this in turn means that there is far less resistance from within the educational system to the influence of these groups.

It is important that we understand the kind of influences which have helped to form and inform such ideologies as those of the Green and New Age movements. Many people today accept at least some aspects of the Green and New Age agenda, though often acceptance of the world-view they represent is subliminal. Nevertheless, the general acceptance of these views is damaging to our culture and to our children in that they help to form a world-view which is essentially pagan in nature. The degree to which the old pre-Christian religion—which has enjoyed a revival in this century—has in-

---

1. The recent case of an educational authority in England that allowed a book to be placed in state primary schools which promoted a homosexual lifestyle as a morally acceptable form of family life is a case in point.

fluenced these movements is not generally appreciated. The following quotation should serve to illustrate this:

> People today are at last beginning to realise the consequences of becoming what Dion Fortune called 'orphaned of the Great Mother'. We are beginning to look at what has happened and is happening to our planet. It has at last registered upon us that whatever utopias are built upon politicians' promises, if the planet itself is ruined such promises can be nothing but wind-blown dust. Our fate is bound up with that of Mother Earth, whose children we are. Hence the emergence of what has come to be called 'Green politics'.
>
> This, in my opinion, is another indication of the oncoming of the Aquarian Age. It is the time when we must understand and use the past in order to build upon it for the future. The Old Religion must look forward also, and continue its evolution. If it does so, it can play a vital role in the New Age. Indeed, paganism in various forms is already beginning to do this.[2]

This quotation is taken from a book called *Witchcraft, A Tradition Renewed.* There are fundamental areas of common ground between witchcraft, or the "Old Religion," as the authors of this book like to call it, and the modern Green and New Age movements. Indeed the revival of the pagan outlook generally has been a stimulus to the growth of the Green and New Age movements.

Futhermore, whereas witchcraft was for centuries a faith that was practised secretly due to the influence of the church and of Christian culture generally, it is today coming out into the open more and more, along with other practices which were endemic in pagan antiquity such as homo- and bisexual practices. The authors cite the present situation as a reason for being more open: "There will certainly be those who will condemn John and myself for 'saying too much', 'giving away

---

2. Evan John Jones and Doreen Valiente, *Witchcraft, A Tradition Renewed* (London: Robert Hale, 1990), p. 11.

secrets' and so on. . . However, I feel that we have to recognise the changing times, and be ready if necessary to change with them."[3] The "vital role" that witchcraft is playing in the birth of the New Age is of sufficient importance for the authors to "ask those who find this book disturbing . . . to consider this aspect of the matter."[4] Thus, we are to bear with the vile acts of witchcraft even if we detest them simply because of the importance it will play in the birth of the New Age, in helping us return to the veneration of "Mother Nature, Gaia, the Magna Mater, Mother Earth,"[5] call her what you will, for "She is, if you like, the Intelligence behind Nature, which is, as it originally was, conceived of as feminine."[6] We are also told that "Her son and consort is the old Horned One whom our primitive ancestors depicted on the walls of their cave-sanctuaries."[7]

One might be tempted to laugh at all this were it not for the fact that such beliefs are becoming more popular in our society. The "Old Religion" is once again coming out of hiding to some degree, and although it is not exactly evangelical in its posture it is certainly more militant in its demand for toleration: "We are at an important turning-point in human history" we are told, and this is "the changeover from the Age of Pisces to the Age of Aquarius." Thus, "Those of us who have preserved the knowledge that is known as 'occult', a word meaning simply 'hidden', now need to make use of that knowledge in a constructive way. Moreover, we have to make a stand against ignorance and bigotry, and for the recognition of our old faith as a legitimate religion."[8]

It is unlikely that we shall have a revival of witchcraft as a coherent set of rituals practiced on a regular basis by any more than a few enthusiasts, but many of the basic religious

3. *Ibid.*
4. *Ibid.*
5. *Ibid.*, p. 10.
6. *Ibid.*
7. *Ibid.*
8. *Ibid.*, p. 12.

and philosophical ideas and presuppositions underpinning it, which were common to ancient paganism and indeed to all forms of paganism, are already widely accepted in our culture.[9] Popular "science"—an absurd combination of scientific speculation, media hype and badly interpreted statistics—has now picked up on many of these ideas and, by baptising them with pseudo-scientific jargon, given them the appearance of respectability. As a result of this they now represent a significant component of modern Western society's eclectic worldview and play an increasingly prominent role in the formulation of political ideologies.

In an article entitled "The Green Man: The Re-emergence of a vital spirit—Father Earth" published in November 1990 in *World Magazine*, a BBC publication, we are informed that "There is no doubt that the Green Man, the dynamic male counterpart to Mother Nature, is once again a force to be reckoned with. Traditionally connected with whatever is most vital in a particular period—fertility in pagan times, creativity in Romanesque and Gothic times, and learning in the Middle Ages—today he coincides with the growing awareness of a need for balance between us and our environment."[10] According to Julian Henriques, the Green Man is "telling us something about our human relationship with the natural world. As an icon embodying ancient Celtic roots, he appears to validate the modern day quest for lifestyles which are more 'natural' than our present eco-destructive and materialistic ones. Indeed, the Norwegian Green Party have focused their anti-acid rain campaign on an image of the Green Man as the protector of the forests."[11] Co-author William Anderson, also

---

9. See G. North, *Unholy Spirits: Occultism and New Age Humanism* (Ft. Worth, Texas: Dominion Press, 1986).

10. Julian Henriques and William Anderson, "The Green Man: The Re-emergence of a vital spirit—Father Earth" in *World Magazine* (November 1990), no. 43, p. 25.

11. *Ibid.*, p. 26.

the author of a book entitled *Green Man: the Archetype of our Oneness with the Earth,* concludes: "Today we are learning to see Earth once more as the Great Goddess, as Gaia, and he, her son, her lover and her guardian, returns to help us, to warn us and to face us with the impossible challenges of living in harmony with Nature."[12]

The appearance of this article coincided with a BBC *Omnibus* film on the Green Man and a fictional television film series about the Green Man. The British Broadcasting Company is certainly no back-street occult publishing house, and *World Magazine* is one of the better quality general interest magazines on sale in Britain. Both the magazine article and the films are an indication of the extent to which such ideas are beginning to filter through into modern Western culture.

The basic premise behind all of this, and behind the Green and New Age movements etc., is that nature is normative, indeed nature is god, and man, if he is to find his true place in the order of things, must recognise and submit to this. Man must cease from acting as lord over nature, the role assigned to him in the Bible, and submit to the lordship of Mother Earth. Man is not seen as created by a transcendent God in His image to rule over the earth, but simply as another part of the pantheistic god Nature, Gaia, or whatever modern man calls it. If the planet is to survive, and man with it—though one cannot help thinking that the latter is not part of the agenda of the Animal Rights groups—then he must submit to the rule of an untamed Mother Nature as normative. He must accept her yoke and submission to the elements of nature rather than take up his proper God-given role as lord over the earth. The basic idea is that man has vaunted himself above his position and in his pride and arrogance has brought the natural world to ruin through overexploitation of the earth's resources etc. Man's lordship over the earth is seen as harm-

12. *Ibid.*, p. 32.

ful, and destructive of the natural order. Man's sin is that he has interfered with nature. We must restore the balance, therefore, and this means returning to the worship of Mother Nature and the acceptance of our position in the pagan order of things.

The Christian perspective

We now see the radical difference between the pagan world-view and that of orthodox Christianity. The pagan view of Nature and man's place in it is utterly idolatrous. Man indeed has vaunted himself above his position, but he has done this by claiming a kind of divinity and usurping the authority of God, not by claiming lordship over the earth. Man *is* lord over the earth under God. That is his rightful position in the divine order of things. His lordship over the earth is legitimate when he submits to God. But by vaunting himself above God and His authority he has brought himself and the natural world into a state of disorder. Man is now under the dominion of sin, which is disobedience to God, until he is redeemed in Jesus Christ, and the earth is under the curse of God as a result of this sin. Of course sin leads men to abuse God's creation, but the answer to this is not man's subjugation to nature, since this is the result of sin.

The Christian answer to man's abuse of the creation is subjection to God and the restoration of man's dominion over nature[13] in Jesus Christ. In Christ man once again submits to

---

13. The word "nature" here means simply the natural world in contrast to the world of those human affairs that are governed by ethics. In this sense nature is simply another term for God's creation. However, the term is used by humanists and pagans to mean an intelligent entity in itself. Thus, the New Age and Green movements have revived the concept of the world soul common in antiquity. Indeed this is the natural outworking of their position. Nature, for the pagan, is a living god and the world and all things in it are aspects of this god. This conception of Nature is pantheistic and animistic, and has a growing following even in the "scientific" West, as is evidenced by

God, and therefore godly dominion over the earth again becomes normative for man and for the natural world. Rather than abusing the world the Christian seeks—or at least should seek—to exploit it to the glory of God and the betterment of mankind. This involves the subjugation and control of the natural world, animate and inanimate. Man is not simply another animal, nor an insignificant part of nature who must learn to live harmoniously with nature if he and the earth are to survive. He is the lord of the earth, and if the earth is to survive he must begin to exercise that lordship in obedience to God and in conformity with His covenant law.

Man's dominion over the earth certainly cannot be achieved by his degrading himself to the level of the animals, but by *ruling over* the earth and the animals and subjecting them to himself as their lord, since this is what God created man for. Man's dominion and mastery over the earth is a major aspect of God's purpose for mankind; but it can only be achieved successfully as man subjects himself to God and seeks that dominion in obedience to His law. This is because the covenant that God has established with mankind, and which defines man's existence, governs the whole of man's life, thoughts and actions: it governs not only man's vertical relationship to his Creator, but also his horizontal relationship to the created order, to the world of men and things. Thus, a break in the vertical relationship between God and man through man's sin and rebellion against God leads to a perverting and overturning of the horizontal relationship between man and the world in which he lives.

This is why all forms of paganism lead to the subjugation

---

the occult and New Age movements. For the Christian this concept of nature is idolatrous. Nature, or the natural world, is the arena of man's dominion, not God. Natural law for the Christian, therefore, would refer simply to those second causes by means of which God governs the natural world, God's laws of nature, in contrast to ethical law, which governs man's life as a moral creature responsible to God for his thoughts and actions.

of man to the world around him rather than to the subjecting of the world to the rule of man. Paganism in all its forms involves, indeed is based upon the worship of the creation rather than the Creator. And that which man worships he puts himself in subjection to. He thus becomes the slave of that which he worships. Worship of the natural world, therefore, leads to man's bondage to the elements of nature, and therefore to the death of man and the death of civilisation.

Whenever man rejects allegiance and service to his Creator and attempts to cast away God's binding covenant he subjects himself to some aspect of the created order as the governing principle of life, rather than to the infallible word of God. All such rebellion, irrespective of its religious language and symbolism, or lack of it, is a return to paganism, and its end is the enslavement of man to the creation. This is evident in such diverse forms of paganism as Marxist communism on the one hand, which claims "scientific" status through its appropriation of the language of economics and sociology, and the pagan religions and mystic cults of the ancient world, so evidently revived in the New Age movement of today, on the other.

Classic paganism

As an illustration of the power and the devastating effects of fallen man's bondage to the created order we shall look briefly at one classic example of such paganism: Hinduism. The fact that Hinduism has been practised for so long and is so ingrained in the culture of the Indian sub-continent affords a perspicuous and revealing instance of the effects of paganism on both human society and the natural world, and a sobering glimpse of man's future under the influence of the neo-pagan revival.

For the Hindu the cow is sacred, a well as other animals such as the monkey. These animals roam freely over the land

and destroy valuable crops grown for human consumption.[14] But they are considered sacred and therefore Hindus refuse to drive them away from their crops for fear of their gods. The Hindus refuse to take dominion over the world and over the animals that roam over the earth, and hence their crop production is irrational. The result is that crops desperately needed for human survival are destroyed and consumed by animals. The problem is far greater than simply the veneration of the cow however. Professor P. T. Bauer, Britain's leading development economist, states the matter clearly: "A large proportion of the Indian population object to the killing of animals. Besides its immediate and direct affects on the food supply, this attitude obviously restricts the scope of animal husbandry, severely circumscribes agricultural operations and obstructs progress in agriculture. An extreme example is that of the Jains, a considerable sect, adherents of which will not knowingly take any form of animal life, even that of insects and bacteria. They object to the killing of locusts, to the use of insecticides, and even to such measures as the chlorination of water designed to kill the agents or carriers of cholera, typhoid or malaria and other fatal or debilitating diseases of people, livestock and vegetation."[15] Another serious effect of this idolatrous attitude to the natural world can be seen in the fact that rats at the docks consume up to fifty per cent of India's annual food imports.[16]

The Hindu thus becomes enslaved to the world around him, and he is at its mercy. And this is because he worships the creature rather than the Creator, and refuses to act in obedience to his Creator and take dominion over the earth and over the animals. He is thus ruled by the world which he

---

14. P. T. Bauer, *Indian Economic Policy and Development* (London: George Allen and Unwin Ltd., 1961), pp. 23-25.

15. *Ibid.*, p. 23.

16. David Chilton, *Productive Christians in an Age of Guilt Manipulators* (Tyler, Texas: Institute for Christian Economics, third edition 1985), p. 119.

was given to rule over. Having made gods of his environment and the animals that God has commanded him to subjugate for his own advancement and advantage in the service of God, he has become subject himself to his environment. His life is governed by a servile relationship to the natural world, rather than the natural world being utilised in a godly and productive fashion for his own benefit and the benefit of mankind *and* the animal kingdom.

Under the British Raj India was a net exporter of food.[17] Independence brought a drastic change, as can be seen from the title of an official document published in 1959 called *India's Food Crisis.*[18] P. T. Bauer has pointed out that "even in the favourable year of 1958-59 there were still food riots, while in 1957-58 acute shortages were widespread."[19] Legislation prohibiting the slaughter and sale for slaughter of cattle, and the sale and transportation of beef products in any form, was passed in 1956.[20]

This is institutionalised paganism, and its end is the subjugation of man to the natural world, with all the poverty, social backwardness and human misery associated with it. Such effects are always to be found as the natural outworking of paganism. Hinduism, like all other pagan religions, is the overturning of God's created order and of man's God-ordained place in it, and thus Satanic in its nature and effects. Man, who should be lord over the earth, is enslaved to the natural world, which is allowed to run wild, and thus at its mercy, rather than taming it as God intended him to do.

All things suffer under such a religion. Man suffers: he lives in poverty and a state of semi-starvation through underutilisation and management of the resources available to him. The natural world, which was created for man's stewardship

17. *Ibid.*
18. P. T. Bauer, *op. cit.*, p. 67.
19. *Ibid.*
20. *Ibid.*, p. 23f.

and thus which is normative only under his management, becomes a semi-wilderness, and fails to achieve its full potential, since this also is dependent on the godly exploitation and management of its resources by mankind (Gen. 2:15).

The effects of paganism and Christianity contrasted

Whenever and wherever man refuses to take godly dominion over the earth according to God's revealed covenant law human bondage and suffering is the result. When man refuses to be the servant of God, and as a result lord over the earth, he makes himself the servant of the creation rather than of the Creator and thus comes under bondage to the natural world. Thus men starve to death in a world of plenty created by a God of bounty. And this is because man refuses to live under God and His law. For there is space and food enough in this world for all who now live or ever will live on it, if only man will use the earth productively and obediently in accordance with God's revealed word. But fallen man would live in autonomy from God and die rather than serve the God of creation and live.

As God's servant man stands in the privileged position of being God's vicegerent over the earth and thus lord of the natural world. As a rebel against God he enslaves himself to the world he was meant to rule over. Sin, rebellion against God, overturned the created order not only between man and his Creator, but also between man and his environment (Gen. 3:17-19). This is because the covenant that God has established with mankind is all-embracing: it defines not only man's relationship to God, but also, as we have already seen, his proper relationship to the world around him. Thus to break the covenant and rebel against it is to pervert and destroy not only man's relationship with the Creator but also his proper, God-ordained relationship with the creation.

When man rejects his Creator as his Lord and Sovereign and idolises some aspect of the created order instead he ceases to be God's legitimate vicegerent and lord over the natural world. His dominion turns into the *domination* of some men over others, and his idolatry leads to the subjugation of all men to the created order. The power of sin over mankind, its ability to enslave mankind, is thus very real and the cause of the wretched conditions and human misery prevalent in so much of the world.

This is why it is only as the Christian religion has advanced over the last two thousand years, and especially since the Reformation, that starvation, disease, human misery and suffering, as well as tyranny[21] and material slavery, have been overcome to any significant degree, for Christianity restores man's relationship with God and thus his proper relationship with the created order. The parts of the world where such slavery and bondage is still great are those where Christianity has had least influence.[22] Truly, the Christian faith has brought freedom and release to a world which was in bondage to pagan-

21. In Europe where such tyranny has reared its head it has been the concommitant of ideologies which have self-consciously rejected the Christian religion, e.g. Marxism, and in the case of Nazism even a self-concious return to occult paganism.

22. I do not include Roman Catholicism here in the term Christianity. It is clear that the Roman Catholic Church today is non-Trinitarian and syncretistic to the core. Indeed, in many places where Roman Catholicism has flourished natives have simply added the Roman Catholic God to their pantheon of idols. Thus, in Central and South America Roman Catholicism and primitive animistic cults exist side by side and are practised equally by the natives. In some instances the Roman Catholic Church has not even attempted to extirpate idolatry and has simply presented accommodated forms of Christian symbols which function as alternative or rather complimentary idols for the population. The result is a similar kind of situation to Aaron's presentation of the golden calf to the Israelites as a valid representation of their God. In this way the Roman Catholic Church has proved itself to be essentially a pagan religion. Thus the distinctive effect of social amelioration experienced by those cultures which have come under the influence of the Christian religion has significantly lagged behind where Roman Catholicism has been the ma-

ism and all the misery and death that goes with it. "If the Son therefore shall make you free, ye shall be free indeed." (John 8:36)

The natural order

The humanist wants to be free from God, but that means the enslaving of men. The Green movement, Animal Rights people etc. want the natural world to be free from man's rule and dominion over it, but that means that man is at the mercy of nature and thus in bondage to it. Thus freedom and servitude for man are not absolutes which he can or must choose between. Man cannot escape his creaturely limitations and hence can never be totally free in the sense that he can determine his own destiny without reference to the God who created him and the creation he is part of and in which he finds his true purpose and meaning. The question facing man is therefore not whether he should choose freedom on the one hand or servitude on the other—servitude in one form or another is an inescapable fact of life for man—but *whom* shall he serve and in *what* does his true freedom, his original God-ordained freedom, consist?

The humanists, Green movement and New Age people want man to be free from God and His law so that they can determine for themselves what constitutes man's true nature and place in the world. They want to re-create themselves and the world around them according to their own images and idols. But this brings them into bondage in one form or another to the world or the aspects of it which they have idolised. This is completely contrary to the God-created order of life and the creation mandate that God has given to man. Man is to *rule over* nature and serve *God* thereby. His true freedom

---

jor religious influence. Even Western European countries where Roman Catholicism has traditionally been strong have lagged behind their Protestant neighbours in terms of general social and economic advancement.

consists in the fulfilling of his God-created purpose in life, and this is only possible as he submits to God in obedience to His word. To serve the living God is the only true freedom man can know. To rebel against God means bondage and slavery for man.

The end of humanism and all other forms of paganism, including the Green and New Age movements etc., is the subjugation of man to the world around him—the enslaving of men to each other and to the elements of nature—and hence the death of man and the destruction of civilisation. For nature is *not* normative; it is not the *natural* God-ordained order of things. Nature is wild and untamed without man to rule over it. It was never created to be left to itself, but for man to manage it. A *wilderness* is the result of man's abdication of his responsibility to rule over the earth. And in a wilderness man cannot survive, he must starve. The natural order of things, the God-ordained order, is for man to rule over nature, to take dominion over the earth and over the animals. His true purpose and thus his happiness and prosperity can only be found in obedience to that calling, since that is God's will for him and his duty to God.

It is vitally important, therefore, that Christians proclaim the moral and covenantal nature of human life and work to develop an educational philosophy, anthropology and ethics which is based on that covenant at all points. The Green and ecology movements have so far waged a successful propaganda war. And indeed, some elements of what they say are correct, since man should steward the earth responsibly and look after it. But the underlying philosophy is anti-theistic, anti-covenantal, and thus anti-human because it is pro-nature in the sense that nature is seen as normative. Christians must make it clear that this is not so. Man's dominion over the earth under God is normative—that is to say the original God-ordained order of things—not his subjugation to it. Subjugation to the natural world means death for man, and as the pagan world-view is promoted and gains credence in our society, and is passed on to future generations through the educational system, our civilisation will come under bondage to the elements of nature; it will become pagan in every sense, and judgement and death will be its just reward.

Religion and civilisation

A civilisation's culture is clearly an outworking of its basic religious presuppositions. Culture is religion externalised. Civilisation is thus religiously determined, as Henry Van Til argued in his book *The Calvinist Concept of Culture*.[23] The case of India, as we have already seen, bears ample testimony to this truth. Examples of backward civilisations based on pagan religious world-views could be multiplied throughout the world.[24] By contrast the overriding influence in the West historically has been the Christian religion. Western civilisation and culture has largely been an outworking of Christian ideals and influences.

This is not to say that there have not been other influences upon the West from outside of the Judaeo-Christian tradition. There have been, in particular, influences from the Graeco-Roman world which have helped to shape Western culture. But even these influences have not appeared in the West stark naked in their original form, but have themselves been modified and moulded in accordance with Christian beliefs throughout the history of the West. On the whole Western culture has been influenced by a strong Christian understanding of the

23. Henry Van Til, *The Calvinist Concept of Culture* (Grand Rapids, Michigan: Baker Book House, 1959), p. 8.

24. See Stanley L. Jaki, *Science and Creation: From eternal cyles to an oscillating universe* (Edinburgh: Scottish Academic Press). Jaki demonstrates that science was either absent or still-born in all ancient pagan cultures due to the prevailing religious view of time as cyclical in nature. In contrast science in the Western world emerged from a Christian cultural matrix informed by the biblical view of time as linear, thus providing a conceptual basis for progress.

nature and meaning of life.

Thus, democracy,[25] which is not a peculiarly Christian idea, became in the West a particular kind of democracy, heavily informed by Christian principles and ideals. This is demonstrated by the fact that virtually all attempts by modern Western governments to implant Western democratic ideals into non-Christian cultures have failed miserably. Western style democracy simply breaks down in pagan cultures because they do not have the basic Christian ideals of due process of law, freedom, morality, justice, compassion and mercy etc., which have characterised Western culture under the influence of Christianity and which are thus essential to the existence of a stable democratic system of the type found in the West.[26] It has taken over a millennium for the Western democratic process to develop into its modern form. It is simply not realistic to expect it to take root overnight in a pagan culture which has not yet been emancipated from the worship of the natural world. Indeed, even India, in spite of the fact that it is the largest democracy in the world and benefited greatly from the civilising influence of the British Raj in the last century, has not been able to pull itself into the twentieth century after the pattern of Western culture and achieve the standard of living enjoyed by Western society today. In some respects it has re-

---

25. It should be observed, however, that the English parliamentary system did not develop under the influence of Greek thought. There is no real comparison between early Greek democracy and English parliamentary government. The English parliamentary system developed over hundreds of years and did not come into recognisable form as such until the seventeenth century, and this took place under the overriding influence of Puritan thinking, which itself relied heavily on *biblical* precedents. Government by elected representatives was sanctioned by reference to the election of rulers in Israel and elders in the New Testament church. Thus, at least in England, and America also, which has its political and legal roots in England, parliamentary government developed under the influence of Judaeo-Christian ideals.

26. The extent to which the West is now abandoning these Christian ideals means that the survival of Western democracy is uncertain, indeed unlikely, in its present form.

gressed. And this is largely due to the prevailing religious culture.

Western civilisation after the Reformation

What has been said above regarding the dominant influence of Christianity in Western culture has been particularly relevant since the Reformation. As a result of the Reformation the Bible was translated into the vernacular of the Protestant nations. This led to a far greater influence of Christian principles and ideals in Protestant Europe. The Reformation was the great watershed in the transition of Western culture from feudalism to a modern civilisation.

The Protestant faith placed a high priority on *understanding* the faith and thus on *teaching* the faith to the people. Hence the translation of the Bible into the vernacular. By contrast Roman Catholicism encouraged the people to place their trust in the church and its professional priests, and to rest in these as the means of salvation. Understanding the faith did not have the same importance; what counted was the mass—in effect a magical rite—and the merit of the saints etc. The Protestant faith placed the emphasis back on the biblical principles of grace operating through personal faith. This demanded understanding on the part of the believer.

This emphasis on personal faith and understanding, in contrast to the Roman Catholic reliance on the church in which understanding the faith was seen as the duty of the priests and discouraged among the laity, accounts in large measure for the great transformation in Protestant European culture after the Reformation. The rationalisation of life in many ways was the result. Max Weber's thesis concerning the rationalisation of economic enterprise after the Reformation due to the development of a distinctively Protestant understanding of the *calling* gives us an example of the kind of change this produced in the area of work ethics and economics.[27]

In England the result of this shift in emphasis from the church and its professional priesthood to the Protestant principle of the priesthood of all believers, with the concomitant necessity that all believers be taught and understand their duty to God and their calling in the world as a means of rendering a rational service to God (Rom. 12:1), was the conversion of the nation and the transformation of society. Men were discouraged from wallowing in ignorance and trusting in the superstitions and magical rites of the Roman Catholic Church for salvation. They were encouraged instead to *understand* the faith, and to live and act in the light of that understanding in every part of their lives. Sacerdotalism and sacramentalism were no longer considered the content of the Christian religion. The church and its role, even its nature, were demythologised and *teaching* replaced the performance of magical rites as the church's duty before God and responsibility to the people.

There was thus a fundamental shift in the understanding of the church's role. Under Roman Catholicism the church embraced much of paganism, though it was heavily syncretised with the Roman Catholic understanding of the Christian faith. In the Roman Catholic Church salvation was understood to be administered to the lay members of the church by the magical manipulations of a professional priesthood. Protestantism instead turned to teaching the faith to the people so that they might shoulder their responsibilities in the world as God's people, bringing His word to bear on all aspects of their life. This led to the transformation of life and culture in all areas. Since the Christian faith is relevant to the whole of life, an understanding of man's calling and duty in terms of the purpose of God was extended to the whole of life.

---

27. Max Weber, *The Protestant Ethic and the Spirit of Capitalism* (George Allen and Unwin, 1930).

This educational emphasis of the Reformation had an immense effect on the whole of Protestant culture. It went beyond the limits of "religious" education in the narrower sense, or theological education, to embrace the whole of life and society. Furthermore, the world is God's creation and a revelation of His eternal power and Godhead (Rom. 1:20), and therefore to be understood by the believer no less than God's revelation of Himself in Scripture. More properly, the Protestant view was that the natural world was to be understood *through* the teaching of Scripture. In this way all things were brought under the authority of God's word and the rule of Christ for the glory of God.

The effect of this revival of biblical Christianity was the birth of modern Western society, a renewed Christian civilisation characterised by the growth of learning and science,[28] exploration and world mission, social amelioration etc. This transformation of Western civilisation was brought about by the opening up of men's minds to the world around them and their place and duty in it as men with a calling to bring all things into obedience to God's word. Protestants opened schools and colleges which challenged the quality and superiority of even the old established universities, especially in terms of *applied* learning, science and technology, which lagged behind in the old universities for many years. Protestant education was a major factor in the transformation of our nation from a feudal society to a modern industrial civilisation.

---

28. The growth of science is wrongly attributed to the Renaissance by many. Frances Yates has shown that the Renaissance was characterised not by the birth of modern science but by a revival of ancient occult "science." Kabbala was the great fetish of the men of the Renaissance, who were thus not scientists in the modern sense so much as occult mystics. The Renaissance revived not ancient Greek science—which was negligible in any case (see Jaki, *op. cit.*)—but rather ancient pagan occultism (see Frances A. Yates, *Giordano Bruno and the Hermetic Tradition* [University of Chicago Press (1964) 1991], *The Occult Philosophy in the Elizabethan Age* [Routledge and Kegan Paul, 1979, Ark edition 1983]).

Our civilisation is, or at least has been, largely a Christian civilisation, and a Christian civilisation can only take root and flourish where men are taught to understand the Christian faith and its implications for the whole of life and culture. Christian civilisation necessitates a Christian world- and life-view, and the working out of that world-view in the totality of life, both on the individual and on the societal levels.

Medieval Christendom was vitiated in this respect due to its virtual denial of the priesthood of all believers and its limiting of the nature of Christian priesthood to the ecclesiastical and theological spheres. The sharp contrast between the sacred and the secular which characterised medieval Christendom meant that the application of God's word to much of life was neglected. Secular callings were not seen as priestly callings and thus the dominant influence of Christian principles in those spheres was missing. This was so among academic disciplines also. Philosophy, for instance, in spite of the fact that it was the domain of the medieval church, was seen as a discipline governed by neutral rational principles. The intellect was deemed to be unfallen essentially and thus instead of subjecting all philosophical thought to the authority of God's word the idea of autonomous human rationality was accepted and natural theology and Aristotelian philosophy dominated the discipline. The influence of the church was certainly very great upon society, but the influence of the Christian faith was limited in comparison to post-Reformation Europe, since its sphere of operation was seen as being almost exclusively ecclesiastical. Christian culture therefore failed to develop properly. Instead there was regression, and then regression turned to oppression and Roman Catholic tyranny developed as the church became increasingly corrupt.

Only after the Reformation was Western society able to develop into a more consistently Christian culture. With the Protestant understanding of the *calling* and the redemption of all spheres of life and activity as a means of serving God according to His word society experienced a practical outworking of the Christian faith which led to greater progress across the whole spectrum of human life and activity, not the least of which was social and economic amelioration on a grand scale. The emphasis that the Reformation church placed on understanding and education, and on man's divine calling in the world, played an important role in this process, and the growth of education generally was also a result of it.

Contemporary Western culture

Today we have largely, though not yet totally, abandoned the Christian religion as the basis of our way of life, our culture. It survives nominally in our institutions because tradition dies hard. But as an animating cultural force it has gone. Unfortunately, the church, due to the dominating influences of pietism and escapism among the Reformed and evangelical churches, and liberalism in the larger Protestant denominations, has provided no resistance to the secularising influences of modern humanism. Christian education has virtually ceased in the church and has been handed over lock, stock and barrel to the secular humanist state. In all but a few cosmetic details Church of England schools, for instance, are simply state schools with virtually no distinctively Christian philosophy or practice in the education they provide.

Christian civilisation has declined as secular humanism has advanced in this way. Slowly but surely in one area after another the church has surrendered to the humanist hordes: first it surrendered the sovereignty of God, then history, then morality, and now it is on the brink of surrendering the very faith itself, indeed in most large denominational colleges it has already done so—the progression is logical once God's sovereign jurisdiction over man's life is denied. The old Enlightenment humanism itself, which at least paid lip service to the Christian faith, is now in decline and in its place a more virulent and self-conscious neo-paganism is beginning to dominate our culture. It is not uncommon today to hear Church of England ordinands express doubts as to the exclusive validity of the Christian faith, and pagan religions are entertained as valid ways of seeking God etc. In large measure these developments can be traced to the decline of Christian education in our land at all levels, in the home, in schools and at college and university.

In the light of this fact the provision of Christian education must surely be seen as one of the main tasks to be undertaken by the Christian church today in its commission to bring the nation under the discipline of Christ (Matt. 28:19-20). Without a specifically Christian philosophy and practice of education the nation will not ultimately be disciplined to Christ. Education is of central significance in any culture. The religious principles underpinning the prevailing philosophy of education in any society will determine that society's world-view. Education is of central importance in the transmission of a civilisation's understanding of the nature and meaning of life to the next generation, and thus for the preservation of that civilisation's way of life. Without the revival of a specifically *Christian* philosophy and practice of education as a means of transmitting our way of life to our children, Christian civilisation will be extinguished in our land within the next few generations. It is impossible to Christianise a culture without providing an education for that culture which is based on a Christian world-view. Christian civilisation necessitates Christian education, at every level and in every field, at home, church, school and college.

Conclusion

It is through the education of our children that our world-view is passed on to future generations and our civilisation thereby preserved. Christians, therefore, have a very simple choice: either they educate their children in terms of godly learning and discipline and a Christian world-view, a covenantal, dominion oriented world-view, and thereby help to build and preserve Christian civilisation, or they hand over the education of their children to pagans who will educate them in terms of ungodly learning and discipline and a pagan world-view, and thereby help to build a pagan civilisation which will enslave their children to the world they are called to rule over.

To quote Rushdoony again: "Man creates by the totality of his life and actions a culture; it is the visible form of his faith and life. The question therefore is, what kind of culture will he produce?"[29] Either we educate our children in terms of a Christian culture, or we hand them over to be educated by humanists as pagans. Our actions in this matter will help to determine and shape the culture of the next generation. Either we build in terms of the Christian faith, or we destroy the Christian culture our forefathers built: "He who is not with Me is against Me; and he who does not gather with Me scatters" (Matt. 12:30). Education is the single most important factor in the preservation of a society's culture. On the education of our children the future of our civilisation hangs.

It is the Christian's duty to educate his children in the Christian faith for dominion, for the shouldering of man's creation mandate to bring the whole earth into subjection to himself as God's steward and vicegerent on earth, and thus into subjection to God and His word. This necessitates a Christian culture and the building of Christian civilisation, and this in turn necessitates a Christian, covenantal, dominion oriented philosophy and practice of education.

---

29. R. J. Rushdoony, "Calvinism and Culture" in *Calvinism Today*, vol. I, no. 1 (January, 1991), p. 5*b*.

7

SOME OBSERVATIONS ON THE ROLE OF THE CHURCH IN THE PROVISION OF EDUCATION

I stated in the Introduction that it is vitally important that the *church* should take a positive stance over the issue of education, that it should make a determined and sustained effort to reverse those trends within the church which militate so much against the provision of Christian education, and that it should begin promoting and facilitating to the best of its ability a programme of re-education in this vitally important area. This needs to be clarified now and the proper role and place of the church in the area of education examined.

(1) State education and the church

First of all, it cannot be emphasised too strongly that from the biblical point of view education is *not* the responsibility of the *state*. Education, as I argued in Chapter Three, is a *family* responsibility. The school is not a divinely ordained institution with a God-given mandate in the field of education. In the Bible the family is the God-ordained institution with responsibility for the education of its members. Thus, the state, which in the Bible is a ministry of *justice*, exceeds its God-given authority when it takes upon itself the task of setting educational standards and making provision for education through state-run and state-funded schools. For the state to require compliance with such standards or to enforce attendance at state-run or regulated schools is *tyranny.* There is no Welfare State in the Bible. Welfare is the responsibility of the family primarily, and where the family is unable to provide it becomes the responsibility of the church. Education is an aspect of the family's welfare responsibility, and thus only when the family is no longer able to make suitable provision does it become the responsibility of the church—but *never* does it become the responsibility of the state.

State control and funding of education by means of tax revenues is a hammer blow against the Christian faith, since by controlling the provision of education according to its own standards and philosophy the state usurps the parents' God-given responsibilities, and by financing state education with taxes it not only breaks the eighth commandment but also vitiates the ability of parents to provide for their children's education outside of the state system. This situation is exacerbated for those who do not use the state system by the fact that the funding of state education by tax revenues has made state education free *at the point of delivery* and thereby effectively ruined the market for private education. Thus only the wealthier members of society can afford to pay the fees charged by public schools.

Were the state to withdraw from education all together not only would parents have more resources available for their children's education—assuming of course that the state reduces tax rates accordingly—but the market for private education would be healthier, more varied and more efficient from the economic point of view. The provision of education would also be geared to the demands of customers with a realistic view of the product supplied, rather than the population being at the mercy of the latest whims and pet theories of state supported academics and bureaucrats. The resulting situation would be more advantageous to all and from every point of view. Consumer choice and competition between suppliers would maximise quality and minimise costs since education would be a commodity on sale in the market like any other economic good.

The role of the church in this matter should be to provide biblical teaching on the proper function of the state and the limits of its authority. Christians should be taught to observe these boundaries laid down in Scripture and steered away from state education. The church should encourage the establishing of new Christian schools and colleges and the development of those already in existence. Our aim should be to create a situation in which education is free from all forms of state funding and control. In the interim, while state and private schools co-exist, Christian schools should be encouraged to resist all state interference with their work and refuse all state support in the form of grants etc. Christian schools and parents should not rely on state funding in any way.

(2) The role of the church under normal circumstances

Neither is the *church* the God-ordained institution responsible for the education of children in the first instance. Again, we must stress that education is the responsibility of the *family*, and therefore parents must either obtain services offered by private schools which will provide an education that is consistent with the teachings of the Christian faith or provide for their children by means of home schooling. The primary role of the church is the ministry of the word and sacraments. As a general rule the church should not, under *normal* circumstances, finance or subsidise the education of children.[1]

1. As part of its ministry of the word, however, the church needs to train church leaders and ministers, and church-run theological colleges and training centres dedicated to this purpose are quite legitimate *in principle*—though whether the kind that generally exist today in Britain are valid ex-

Church welfare and evangelism

There are, however, two exceptions to this general rule in which education may come under the proper role of the church in the exercise of its ministry: (1) Part of the church's ministry is to help the poor and needy, and heal the sick. Thus, the church does have a welfare role to play in helping those in need. It needs to be stressed, however, that the role of the church as a dispenser of welfare is related to the *needy*, the poor and destitute, and those who are unable to help themselves. The role of the church in this area is charitable in nature. Education, as an aspect of welfare, may on occasions come under the church's ministry in this area.

There are three ways in which the church may provide for this: first, church-sponsored and church-run schools may be established. This may be in the context of a wider ministry to the needy such as homes for orphans, destitute single mothers, families genuinely living in poverty etc. Thus church schools and orphanages may work together in the context of the church's overall ministry. Second, the church could provide scholarships to independent Christian schools for the children of families in need. Third, interest free loans could be

---

amples of this principle is another question. In training ministers there is only a certain amount that can be done effectively in the college environment, and perhaps too much stress is placed on the college system for training ministers today, resulting in many cases in churches being led by academics out of touch with the real world and unable to minister to the needs of the church in today's world. The college system also tends to foster an unrealistic ethos of pietism which sets ministers apart from ordinary people and this must surely account for so many of the problems that ministers face today in managing churches, as well as their inability to relate to people in a down to earth way. However, theological education is very necessary for those involved in church ministry and leadership and this may be provided, among other ways, in church-run colleges—though it cannot escape one's notice that so many who do attend theological college today seem to acquire very little in the way of a sound theological education. In principle, though, church-run theological colleges are a legitimate and abiding part of the church's ministry under normal circumstances.

made to families in need to enable them to provide for their children's education either through fee paying Christian schools or by means of home schooling. For instance, where financial straits necessitate that both parents work, but where income is still insufficient to enable school fees to be paid, an interest free loan could be made either to place the children in a Christian school or to enable one of the parents to stay at home and home-school their children. The parents would decide which was the best course of action according to their circumstances and abilities. This kind of loan should have a maximum repayment limit of seven years, after which any outstanding debt should be cancelled (see Ex. 22:25, Lev. 25:35-36, Deut. 23:19-20 and Deut. 15:1-11).

Where children are still part of a family—i.e. where they are not orphaned—this third option is probably a better way to provide help than by simply providing free schooling or scholarships, since it gives the responsibility for the children's education to the parents, whose duty it is, rather than relieving them of their responsibility. The church then provides help but, by removing as little as possible of the responsibility for the children's education from the orbit of the parents decisions and actions, it strengthens the family structure and parental authority rather than weakening it. A requirement of such loans would be that the schools chosen should operate on the basis of a Christian philosophy and practice of education, or where home schooling is chosen, that choice of curriculum and materials used should be consistent with a Christian view of education. Church-run schools and direct scholarships would then be reserved for orphans.

While this is the preferable way for the church to provide help to families in need the actual course of action taken would be determined by the specific circumstances of individual family needs, and churches would have to determine for themselves which is the best way to proceed in the light of those circumstances. I am not arguing that this should be a hard and fast rule but simply indicating what I think is the best option on the whole. I have arrived at this conclusion by making the primary consideration that of enabling the family to fulfil its God-given responsibilities itself as much as possible rather than taking over those responsibilities for it. Christian charity should always aim at restoring the normal situation.

(2) The church also has a ministry of evangelism and missionary work, and the provision of education may also come under the church's ministry in this area at times. In a missionary situation the provision of education is a legitimate and necessary aspect of the church's task of evangelism.

These two exceptions to the normal situation relate to the believer and to the non-believer respectively. The provision of welfare where the family is unable to provide for itself is a legitimate function of the church in its ministry to believers. The provision of the same to non-believers is also legitimate in the wider context of the church's ministry of evangelism (all provision of welfare from the church to non-believers should be tied to this evangelistic mission since such charity is a means of living out the faith and practically bearing witness to man's salvation in Jesus Christ).

The normal situation

Under normal conditions, however, the family should provide and pay for the education of its own members. Normal conditions here means where the family is not destitute or too poor to make provision for itself and where the church is not engaged in missionary work. Thus under normal conditions Christian education should be provided either by means of home schooling or by private fee paying Christian schools. In the latter case, however, education does not cease to be the responsibility of the family, nor is the duty of parents to be abdicated to the school. Private Christian schools simply provide a service which parents purchase as part of the exercise of their responsibility. The obligation to ensure that such services are in conformity with the Christian philosophy and practice of education still rests upon the parents, who bear the final responsibility for their children's education before God.

(3) The role of the church under special circumstances

So far I have been considering the situation that *should* exist under *normal circumstances.* The question now arises as to whether the existence of abnormal circumstances modifies this, and if so, to what extent? In particular, does the situation we face in Britain today, and indeed generally in Western societies, constitute abnormal circumstances sufficient to bring the church into the role of providing Christian education in any way other than that set forth above? Before answering this question I shall first consider briefly the situation we now face in this country.

The present situation

In Britain all tax payers are forced to pay for the provision of state schooling through their taxes, whether they use the system or not. Notwithstanding the legal requirement of Christian assemblies and the 1988 Education Reform Act's stipulation that religious education in state schools should "reflect mainly Christian religious traditions," the kind of education provided by the state system is not Christian by any stretch of the imagination; indeed the prevailing ethos is that of atheistic humanism. It is not possible, therefore, for Christian parents to fulfil their educational responsibilities according to biblical criteria by sending their children to state schools, even though they have been forced to pay for the state system through their taxes—it is not possible for them to do so from the point of view of the Bible's teaching on politics and economics either, but I shall pass over this here since my primary concern is strictly with the educational aspect of the issue.

Furthermore, as indicated above, the state system has significantly reduced the options available to parents seeking private education for their children by pricing most of its private competitors out of the market. The provision of state education which is free at the point of delivery has meant that few private schools are able to exist that can offer a service which is priced low enough to entice most people to use it.[2] Only the wealthier members of society can afford to educate their children in private and public schools without making a significant financial sacrifice which impinges upon family life in other areas.

A significant proportion of both local and national tax revenues is used to finance state education, and there are no tax refunds for those who do not use the state system. There is a double sting in this situation for those Christians wishing to educate their children outside of the state system: first, they have to pay double, in effect, for their children's education, and second, they are forced to subsidise the education of other people's children in terms of a philosophy of education with which they do not agree and a religious world-view—i.e. secular humanism—in which they do not believe, and with money that should be available to finance the education of their own children in accordance with their beliefs. This situation represents a fundamental injustice perpetrated by the very institution which, above all others, has the God-given responsibility to uphold justice and punish wrongdoing: the state. Thus, by illegitimately venturing into the area of welfare the state has

---

2. In contrast to this, fee paying and church schools in nineteenth century England, *before* the 1870 Education Act, provided the nation with an education which even the working classes could afford and which was, in terms of quality and quantity, above the world average even by today's standards. See E. G. West, *Education and the Industrial Revolution* (London and Sydney: B. T. Batsford Ltd., 1975), Chapters 3 and 4.

not only exceeded its authority but vitiated its own proper function as a ministry of *justice.* The result is that Christians are forced to subsidise a pagan education system as well as fund Christian education for their own children. And this is in a situation where the prevalence of socialism has made society poorer generally, and therefore there is on the whole less disposable income available to Christian parents to provide for their children's education than would be the case under the organisation of society on the alternative Christian model.

The questions we must now answer are these: *first,* does this constitute a special situation? *Second,* if it does, to what extent does it modify the normal role that the church should play? In particular, does the fact that the state is able to subsidise its education programme with tax revenues—i.e. theft—justify the subsidising of Christian education by the church on a greater scale than that set forth above under normal circumstances? To put this another way round we could ask, does the current situation in which the state illegitimately plunders the resources needed by the family to provide for its own in accordance with biblical principles in effect place those families who would not normally be considered poor or in need into the category of the needy, and thus put them within the orbit of the church's welfare ministry? *Third,* does the existence of state-funded education which has subsidised and promoted the re-paganising of our society on a vast scale and contributed to the decline of Christian culture and influence in society mean that the current state of affairs constitutes a missionary situation?

A tentative answer

The solution to this problem—viz. whether and to what extent the church should be involved in the provision of Christian education under *abnormal* circumstances—is not simple and it is perhaps wise to consider the answer we arrive at as to some extent tentative. Here again, it may be that no hard and fast rules can be laid down and that, due to a variety of individual circumstances, the problem may be solved by different people and different churches in different ways.

My own view is that the answer is yes to all three questions to *some* extent, but not in all situations and for all people. The answer, it seems to me, will be determined very much by the individual circumstances of the families and churches involved. I find it difficult to give an unqualified yes, while at the same time it seems quite obvious that in many ways the present situation does constitute special circumstances.

If we answer *no* to these questions, then Christian parents will simply have to struggle to provide a Christian education for their children by means of fee paying private schools or home schooling, and the church would only step in to help where there is poverty and hardship. If we answer *yes*, then there are far more options open to the Christian community. The financing of Christian education will be considered a legitimate use of tithe funds by churches and individuals, and thus church-funded and church-run schools, and independent Christian schools supported by the tithe, will become an alternative to the state system as well as private fee paying schools and home schooling. This is likely to result in far greater participation in Christian schooling than would otherwise be the case, and not only for financial reasons—the feeling of safety in numbers is a real psychological factor for many who are not natural pioneers and who would therefore hesitate to launch out on their own in a home schooling programme for instance.

It should perhaps be observed here that as well as church-run schools, private Christian schools which rely on donations to keep their work going have effectively answered this question positively, since such schools are financed not by the payment of fees or parental donations alone—which typically bring in less than half the funds needed—but by the use of tithe money, which is to be used for Christian ministry, and donations by those who consider the school a worthy charitable cause.

If it is decided that the present circumstances do constitute a special situation for Christian parents it is important that we see this as a temporary situation and work to change these circumstances as soon as possible. Church-run and church-financed schools should probably endeavour to become private schools operating independently of church funding and control as soon as they can.

Missionary opportunities

In the light of the rapid deterioration of state education, both in terms of academic standards and discipline, the present situation does present the church with a valuable missionary ground and an opportunity to reach non-believers and their children through Christian and church schools, and this opportunity is likely to increase significantly in the foreseeable future. Churches and Christian charities should seriously consider the possibilities for mission through the provision of Christian education. The education of non-believer's children should not be subsidised by the tithe or church funds, however, unless there is genuine poverty, and then such provisions that are made by the church should be tied to an agreement that those receiving the help attend church with their children. This may be more difficult to implement where church schools are financed partly by fees and partly by subsidies from church funds. Where this is the case places at schools should be offered to Christian parents first of all, and then, where there are available places, to non-believers who wish their children to attend; but again there should be some stipulation that parents and children attend church.

Where non-believing parents are prepared to pay full fees this stipulation of church attendance may not be possible or advisable, though non-believing parents can still be encouraged to attend. Such parents would be sending their children to Christian schools because they have realised that state education is breaking down and failing to provide a decent education for their children. They value the quality of the education provided by Christian schools above their disbelief. This is where the non-believers' pragmatism can lead to a missionary advantage for the church, since their children, through attending Christian schools, will come under the influence of the Christian world-view and this will bear fruit to some extent in spite of their parents' atheism.

Where an independent private Christian school offers loans or scholarships to non-believers it should of course require church attendance by parents and children. If a loan or scholarship is provided by a church to an independent school this would naturally apply also.

(4) The primary role of the church in education

Finally, a few words about the role of the church in teaching God's word to the congregation are necessary. It is part of the church's responsibility and ministry to teach and encourage its members to begin the Christian reconstruction of our society in all areas of life. Whatever decisions are made about the role of the church in education and the validity of church schools and independent schools supported by the tithe as opposed to private fee paying schools, it is clear that education is the high ground in the Christian's battle with humanism today, and therefore it is vitally important that the church should recognise and fulfil its responsibility to preach the necessity of Christian education and instruct its members in their responsibilities before God to educate their children in a manner consistent with the covenant under which they have been redeemed. And the church must encourage and support those who have already begun the task, whether in private Christian schools or at home.

Unfortunately, rather than support and encouragement, many who do pursue a Christian education for their children are ostracised within congregations, particularly in Reformed and evangelical churches, and criticised by ministers and members alike. That such things should happen is an appalling indictment on the church's ministry. Ministers who behave like this should consider the warning of scripture: "Cursed be the one who does the work of the Lord negligently" (Jer. 48:10).

The church, and particularly the leadership in the church, should support and encourage Christian education. In particular, it should be made clear from the pulpit that state and atheist public education is not an option for Christian parents and that to place one's children in such institutions is a denial of the faith and treason against God. The church, therefore, should be actively promoting the Christian philosophy and practice of education as the only valid and obedient way for Christian parents to educate their children in the faith. This must be the ongoing teaching of the church, whether in a missionary situation or not, since it is an abiding principle of the Christian faith that our children should be brought up and educated in the discipline and instruction of the Christian faith. It is of the greatest importance that the church should remind Christians of their responsibilities and constantly encourage faithfulness in this area.

The primary role of the church in education, therefore, is through its ministry of teaching the word of God. Only as the church begins to fulfil its God-given calling to teach its members their duty in this area shall we begin to see a significant change in the practice of the Christian community generally. Until then the practice of Christian education will remain the activity of a committed few with a pioneering spirit and the motivation to launch out onto the sea of a hostile world against the tide of an apostate church. For the few who do, however, the remnant of the faithful, there is the certainty of ultimate victory in spite of the hardships of the present storm. Such a faith is that which overcomes the world against all odds (1 John 5:4).

Conclusion

It must be our aim to work towards establishing the normal situation described above while at the same time recognising that the reality of the present situation may necessitate special measures to enable Christian parents to provide a godly education for their children. The establishing of church schools and independent tithe-funded Christian schools can help to move us towards a change in overall patterns for the provision of education among Christians—and probably among non-Christians also to some extent in the near future—which are more consistent with biblical principles and criteria. Whether church- and tithe-funded schools are adopted or not our goal must be to establish an alternative Christian philosophy and practice of education and make it available as widely as possible. Before this can happen, however, the church, and particularly its leadership, must change its attitude, and ministers must begin teaching the necessity of Christian education to their congregations. With commitment, motivation and faith in God, whose work it is in which we are engaged, we can be confident that we shall prevail, for the Scripture tells us that a time will come when "the earth shall be full of the knowledge of the Lord as the waters cover the sea" (Is. 11:9).

Appendix A

SCRIPTURE AND THE COVENANTS

"Behold, the days are coming," declares the Lord, "when I will make a new covenant with the house of Israel and with the house of Judah, not like the covenant which I made with their fathers in the day I took them by the hand to bring them out of the land of Egypt, My covenant which they broke, although I was a husband to them," declares the Lord. "But this is the covenant which I will make with the house of Israel after those days," declares the Lord, "I will put My law within them, and on their heart I will write it; and I will be their God, and they shall be My people."

(Jeremiah 31:31-33)

It is a sad fact that many professing Christians today do not take seriously the greater part of Scripture. Three quarters of the Bible has been relegated to virtual obscurity, namely, the Old Testament. It is a common view that the teachings of the Old Testament have been superseded by the teachings of the New and are thus no longer applicable to the Christian life. Old Testament doctrine, particularly the law, is seen as inadequate and barbarous, or at least unsuitable for modern times. This attitude is not confined to the nominal Christians who attend church each week out of habit, a sense of duty, or a desire to maintain tradition. Nor is it an attitude that we find only among the theologically liberal elements of church life.

The fact of the matter is that this view of Scripture has gained a strong influence over the supposedly Reformed and evangelical elements within our churches. I would go even further and say that, to the shame of so-called evangelicals, this attitude is increasingly a characteristic feature of modern evangelicalism.

Of course, most evangelicals would deny this and maintain that they hold to the traditional orthodox view of the infallibility of all Scripture. But this disclaimer is to a great extent merely the paying of lip service to the doctrine of the plenary authority of Scripture. In practice the story is very different. *Practically* Scripture is often abandoned in favour of the wisdom of men. Although this is especially true with regard to the teachings of the Old Testament it is by no means uncommon with regard to those of the New Testament either. This trend can be observed in all aspects of Christian life today. Individually and in the organisation and running of most churches, both administratively and pastorally, fidelity to Scripture is at a low ebb. Most Christians would probably be hard pushed to think of a church today which is not in the midst of some kind of debilitating crisis or controversy, whether due to personality and disciplinary problems or simply bad government of the church by negligent elders and ministers little suited to the task of leadership.

It must be said that this deplorable state of affairs largely boils down to the unwillingness of many Christians to take God's word seriously in its entirety. Indeed, it is not uncommon to find both elders and congregation in open rebellion against God's word, showing disregard and even contempt for the plain teaching of Scripture. Yet if a church is to be built up aright it must be built on the foundation of God's word. If we abandon that foundation, both individually and corporately, in our relationships with each other and in our church life, then judgement will inevitably be the outcome. The state of the church in Britain today is a vivid testimony to this truth.

The spiritual condition of the church today in our nation is appalling, and this is a judgement upon us for our infidelity to God's word. And the primary responsibility for this situation lies with those who are in the positions of leadership.

In view of the seriousness of this situation it is vital that we understand and appreciate the importance of adherence to Scripture. With regard to the New Testament I think most Christians would agree here. In *principle*—though certainly not always in practice—the New Testament is accepted as our guide by most Christians, at least among those who call themselves Reformed or evangelical. It is with regard to the scriptures of the Old Testament that the problem is at its most acute. Many simply do not believe that the Old Testament is important. It is read mostly for the purpose of illustration or analogy, or else its teachings are spiritualised away. The *application* of Old Testament scripture is virtually non-existent in most churches today.

This being the case I shall consider here in very general terms: 1. What the New Testament has to say about the nature of the writings of the Old Testament. 2. Why the scriptures of the Old and New Testaments must be seen as a whole. 3. What it is that the whole of Scripture contains, and 4. Why it is so important that we should understand and apply to our lives and culture the teachings of the whole of Scripture, including the Old Testament.

1. *The New Testament view of Old Testament scripture.* What insights can we gain about the nature and abiding validity of the Old Testament from the writings of the New Testament?

In the *first* place, it is quite clear even from a cursory reading of the New Testament that it is written throughout from the perspective of the Old Testament. The writers of the New Testament were steeped in the scriptures of the Old. They assumed the validity, authority, and trustworthiness of these writings and quoted from them freely. Without question they considered the scriptures of the Old Testament to be inspired by God and therefore infallible. Thus the apostle Peter writes: "But know this first of all, that no prophecy of scripture is a matter of one's own interpretation, for no prophecy was ever made by an act of human will, but holy men of God spoke as they were moved by the Holy Spirit" (2 Peter 1:20-21).

Second, the authors of the New Testament considered the scriptures of the Old Testament to be a revelation of God's grace sufficient enough to lead men to salvation through faith in Christ. The apostle Paul writes to Timothy: "You, however, continue in the things you have learned and become convinced of, knowing from whom you have learned them; and that from childhood you have known the sacred writings *which are able to give you the wisdom that leads to salvation through faith which is in Christ Jesus*" (2 Tim. 3:14-15). Not only are these Scriptures sufficient to lead men to faith in Christ, they are also able to train us and equip us with the teaching and guidance necessary for a life of righteousness and good works, for Paul goes on to say: "All scripture is inspired by God and profitable for teaching, for reproof, for correction, for training in righteousness; that the man of God may be adequate, equipped for every good work" (2 Tim. 3:16-17). The scriptures to which Paul is here referring are quite obviously those of the Old Testament. The early Christians did not have a New Testament. Their Bible consisted entirely of the Old Testament scriptures and their respect for the authority of these writings is indisputable.

These arguments alone ought to be strong enough to rid us of any idea that the writings of the Old Testament are of little importance. But there is more.

Third, and most importantly, Christ Himself validated the scriptures of the Old Testament, and in no uncertain terms declared that their authority was permanent:

> Do not think that I came to abolish the law or the prophets; I did not come to abolish, but to fulfil. For truly I say to you, until heaven

and earth pass away, not the smallest letter or stroke shall pass away from the law, until all is accomplished. Whoever then annuls one of the least of these commandments, and so teaches others, shall be called least in the kingdom of heaven; but whoever keeps and teaches them, he shall be called great in the kingdom of heaven. (Matt. 5:17-19)

Christ teaches quite clearly here that the law and the prophets have permanent validity. Their teachings are therefore applicable to us today no less than to those who lived before Christ. The Christian faith is here firmly established by Christ Himself on the scriptures of the Old Testament.

Thus the authors of the New Testament considered the writings of the Old Testament to be of divine origin, infallible, and therefore authoritative for the Christian era.

Fourth, in his second epistle the apostle Peter speaks about those who twist the Scriptures to their own destruction (2 Peter 3:16). It ought to be said here that the excessive spiritualising of the Old Testament which is so common today does not do justice to its content. The Old Testament is simply not that kind of document. The scriptures of the Old Testament are very down to earth and concrete writings. They were not written to be spiritualised. The earthiness of the Old Testament does not always come over in translation with anything like the force that it has in the original language. Both the language and the content of these scriptures often have a raw impact that we are unable to appreciate through reading many of our translations, especially modern translations. To spiritualise the Old Testament is really to empty it of its true content. Furthermore, such spiritualising was alien to the world-view of the Hebrew nation in those times. The kind of spiritualising that is engaged in today would have been foreign to the Hebrew mind, and thus to read the Old Testament in that way is to miss the significance of what it is saying.

This is not to say that the Old Testament is not useful for

the purpose of illustration and analogy. But it should not be seen *only* in these terms. Its teachings are suitable for concrete application in our times. A proper understanding of the teachings of the Old Testament is vital if we are to recover that truly biblical world- and life-view which is indispensable for an effectual and sustained reconstruction of our lives, churches, and nation in terms of the Christian faith.

2. *The unity of Scripture.* The Scriptures contain the progressive unfolding of God's redemptive special revelation. That revelation finds its completion in the gospel of Jesus Christ. But, the revelation of God's saving grace in Jesus Christ presupposes the revelation that came before Christ, and as we have seen, Christ upheld that revelation and bore witness to its abiding validity. Thus, God's revelation must be seen as a whole; and because the Scriptures are the inspired written record of that revelation the Scriptures themselves must be seen as a whole.

It is of the utmost importance therefore that we do not break up the Scriptures into parts that are still valid and others that are not, or make unwarranted and forced distinctions between them. Christ accepted the Old Testament scriptures and saw His own work as our Redeemer as the continuation and fulfilment of their teachings. The law and the prophets were the foundation upon which He built, and this is so because it is the law and the prophets which speak of the things concerning Christ (Luke 24:27). *To diminish the teachings of the Old Testament is thus to diminish the teachings and work of Christ Himself.*

The Scriptures are a whole, comprising Old and New Testaments, each part of which finds its full significance only in relation to the whole scheme of scriptural revelation. In our interpretation of any single part of Scripture, therefore, we must be guided by the teachings of the whole of Scripture. Only by applying this rule to our reading of Scripture shall we be able to avoid the error of veering off into unbalanced and unbiblical teachings.

3. *The covenantal content of Scripture.* The Scriptures contain the doctrine of the covenant and the history of the covenant. The covenant is God's way of relating to mankind. Man is a covenantal creature and his relationship to God is always in terms of a covenant.

This covenant can and has been described as a treaty.[1] In describing the covenant as a treaty, however, care must be taken not to give the impression that it is the result of a process of bargaining in which God and man come to some kind of compromise with regard to their respective rights and claims against each other. Such a process may be a feature of the treaties that men make between themselves, but there is an essential difference between the treaties of men and the covenant that God has established with His people.[2] The covenant is not a negotiated treaty between God and man, it is a fact of creation, and the terms of the covenant are defined and established by divine authority alone. Man was created as a covenantal being and cannot properly be defined except in terms of his covenantal relationship to God. Man may accept or reject the terms of the covenant but he cannot escape the fact

---

1. On the covenant as a treaty see Meredith G. Kline, *The Structure of Biblical Authority* (Grand Rapids, Michigan: Eerdmans, [1972] 1978).

2. This is not to say that there are no similarities between the covenants or treaties of men and the covenant that God has established with mankind. Indeed, there is a necessary similarity and connection between them. Man's propensity to form treaties is a reflection and a consequence of the fact he is, on the most fundamental level, a covenantal creature—i.e. made in God's image as a moral being and thus subject to God's absolute sovereign law. Hence, although there are differences there are also similarities between God's covenant with mankind and the treaties of men. The latter flow from and are made possible by the former because a treaty between men requires as its foundation the covenantal nature of man. The similarities between the two are rooted in the fact that all men are God's creatures and thus share the same covenantal nature. The difference lies in the fact that as Creator God's relationship to man is of an entirely different order to man's relationship to his fellow man.

of the covenant, nor of his creation as a covenantal being. In other words, he may be a covenant keeper or a covenant breaker, but his relationship to God is inescapably covenantal and he must bear, in life and death, the consequences of his response to that covenant.

The concept of the covenant is central to the teaching of the Bible. If we fail to understand and appreciate the significance of the covenant we shall have failed to understand the Bible. The Scriptures cannot be understood properly except in terms of the covenant. The covenant defines the relationship that exists between God and man and thus also the relationship that exists between man and the rest of creation. The former relationship is expressed in Scripture in terms such as "I will walk among you, and will be your God, and you shall be my people" (Lev. 26:12 cf. 2 Cor. 6:16); the latter in terms of dominion, e.g. "be fruitful and multiply, and fill the earth and subdue it" (Gen. 1:28). The terms of the covenant regulate both of these relationships. Thus, the covenant embraces the whole of man's life.

The covenant that God has established with His people is one of grace and therefore entered into by faith alone. This was so in Old Testament times just as it is today. The Old Testament does not set forth a covenant of salvation by works. The Old Testament believer was saved by grace through faith no less than the Christian today. However, to be under a covenant of grace—in other words, to be saved by grace—means to be under the law of that covenant as a way of life, and this is so *today* just as it was in Old Testament times.

The Old Testament gives us the history of God's covenantal dealings with His people before Christ. It also sets forth the terms, or law, of this covenant for all time, and Christ confirmed this when He said that he had not come to abolish the law but *to cause it to abound* (Matt. 5:17). The New Testament shows us how the covenant is applied in the Christian era. But it is the same covenant renewed in Christ.

The concept of the covenant is something that runs through the whole of Scripture. God established His covenant with the patriarchs and their posterity after them, and He delivered the people of Israel from slavery in Egypt and gave them His law on mount Sinai. But as time passed the people turned away from God and flouted His law. They practiced idolatry and broke the covenant that their forefathers had entered into. The result was judgement, for the law of the covenant sets forth both blessings and promises for the faithful, and cursings and judgements on the unfaithful and rebellious (Deut. 28).

Yet God preserved a faithful remnant of His people that the purpose of God might be established and His promises fulfilled, and afterwards God re-established or renewed His covenant with this faithful remnant. In this way the one covenant of redemptive grace was renewed with succeeding generations as they realised that they had sinned and departed from their God, and subsequently turned back to Him in faith and repentance.

This renewing of the covenant with successive generations gives the impression of various covenants; and of course in one sense it is correct to say that there have been various covenants, e.g. the Abrahamic, Mosaic, Davidic covenants etc. Yet these are different covenants in *form* only, not in *substance.* They are *renewals* of the one covenant under which God redeems His people by His free grace and establishes His rule among them. The new covenant, of which Jeremiah speaks in chapter 31, is the final renewal of this covenant of redemptive grace in Jesus Christ, to whom all previous covenants had pointed, and in whom they found their true meaning and purpose.

Objection. It may be objected here that if the Christian or new covenant is the same covenant that prevailed in Old Testament times, then why is it called a *new* covenant in the Scriptures, and in what sense is it new?

There are of course significant differences and adjustments between the old and new covenants, all of which turn on the fact that the central figure of the one eternal covenant of redemptive grace, Jesus Christ, has now come in the flesh and accomplished the work of redemption in history. These differences are important and it is vital that we understand them. But we must also remember that the *substance* or *content* of the covenant remains the same; it is only the *form* that has changed. The Christian or new covenant, therefore, is the renewal of the same covenant of redemptive grace that prevailed in Old Testament times.

Nevertheless, the fact that Jesus Christ has now come in the flesh and accomplished the redemption of His people in history means that the Christian covenant is a new covenant in a very special sense. There are four ways in which the Christian covenant can be said to be a new or better covenant.

The *first* difference relates to the fact that with the coming of Christ there is a full revelation of God's redemptive purpose: "God, after He spoke long ago to the fathers in the prophets in many portions and in many ways, in these last days has spoken to us by His Son, whom He appointed heir of all things" (Heb. 1:1-2).

God's redemptive purpose was revealed progressively throughout the whole period of Old Testament history. The revelation was not given all at once, but rather unfolded gradually from the promise of deliverance given to Adam after the fall, namely, that the seed of the woman should bruise the serpent's head (Gen. 3:15). There is a promise of deliverance here but the way and the means by which this deliverance would be accomplished is almost totally veiled. This promise is like a seed from which God's redemptive purpose grows. As history unfolds there is also an unfolding of the revelation of God's redemptive grace until finally, with the coming of Christ, we have the full revelation of God's saving grace.[3] Revelation ceased after the apostolic age, therefore, since in Jesus Christ

God's redemptive purpose is fully revealed.

The Christian covenant, therefore, is characterised by the full revelation of God's redemptive purpose in Jesus Christ. The veil has been lifted. We see more clearly than did the patriarchs and the prophets, and the canon of Scripture is closed because God's revelation of Himself and of His saving grace is disclosed fully in Jesus Christ.

The *second* way in which the Christian covenant is a new or better covenant relates to the sacrificial law of the old covenant. The sacrificial law regulated the sacrifices and ceremonies which took place under the old covenant. It set forth the necessity for an act of atonement before sin could be forgiven. It specified what was acceptable as an offering and regulated the way in which that offering was to be made. It also specified who could officiate at these ceremonies, namely the priests.

These sacrifices typified Christ, as did also the priest who administered them. We are told in the epistle to the Hebrews that "it is not possible for the blood of bulls and goats to take away sin" (Heb. 10:4). It was not the sacrifice of these animals themselves that took away the people's sins, therefore, but the fact that they prefigured and thus found their true meaning in Christ, whose one act of atonement does take away sins. By faith they received the promise of Christ and His work of atonement, and hence forgiveness of sin, though this was ad-

---

3. In saying that there is development or growth in the content of biblical revelation I am not implying that there is in any sense a development or evolution in the mind of God. To suggest this would be quite unbiblical. God knows the end from the beginning, and He knows the end form the beginning because He has planned the end from the beginning (Is. 46:10). God is totally self-conscious, self-contained and omniscient; there is no growth or development in His knowledge either of Himself or of His creation. But there is development in the historical process of revelation. In times past God spoke through the prophets in many ways, but He has now spoken finally in His Son, and God's redemptive purpose is fully revealed in Jesus Christ. On the progressive nature of biblical revelation see Geerhardus Vos, *Biblical Theology* (Edinburgh: The Banner of Truth Trust, [1948] 1975).

ministered to them under the form of a shadow or type of the Lamb of God.

It is of course true that Christ's atoning work on the cross was veiled in these ceremonies and sacrifices and therefore that the people did not see clearly that to which they pointed. Yet the fact that the full revelation of God's saving grace in Jesus Christ did not come until He came as a man and dwelt among us does not alter the *substance* or content of the earlier revelation, and obedience springing from faith in God, who alone stipulates what is an acceptable sacrifice for sin, is what is required of God's people. Without faith these sacrifices meant nothing. Salvation came to believers in the Old Testament no more by the works of the law than it does to the Christian today. Salvation was always and only by God's grace in Christ through faith. The difference between the Old Testament believer and the New Testament believer is only in the fact that before Christ's incarnation His atoning sacrifice for sin was set forth and administered in a veiled fashion under the sacrifices and ceremonies which form the content of the sacrificial law.

Now that Christ has come and accomplished His work of redemption in history these sacrifices have been fulfilled in His one act of atonement on the cross. The priesthood which administered these sacrifices has also been fulfilled in Christ. His one act of atonement and reconciliation has permanent validity. The observation of the ceremonies and sacrifices has therefore now ceased. But the *substance* of the sacrificial law is still valid, namely, that "without the shedding of blood there is no forgiveness" (Heb. 9:22). The difference now is that Christ has shed His blood once and for all time. The purpose or meaning of the sacrificial law has, therefore, been realised finally in Christ's death.

Since the coming of Christ, therefore, the sacrificial law is observed only when we look to Jesus Christ in faith and put our trust in His atoning sacrifice for sin on our behalf. Thus, the substance or content of the covenants with respect to the necessity for an atonement for the forgiveness of sins and reconciliation with God is the same, but in the Christian covenant the efficacy of the one who makes that atonement is new and everlasting.

Third, although the *substance* of the new covenant is the same as that of the old, since the coming of Christ and the pouring out of the Holy Spirit at Pentecost the *dynamic* is new. The prophets had promised that a time would come when God would pour out His Spirit on all mankind. Joel says:

> And it will come about after this that I will pour out My Spirit on all mankind; and your sons and your daughters will prophesy, your old men will dream dreams, your young men will see visions, and even on the male and female servants I will pour out My Spirit in those days. . . And it will come about that whoever calls on the name of the Lord will be delivered. (Joel 2:28-32)

Isaiah says: "My salvation is about to come and My righteousness to be revealed" (Is. 56:1). There are of course many more prophecies which say the same thing. The coming of Christ was the great event to which the prophets of the Old Testament had looked forward. Now that Christ had come all these prophecies were being fulfilled. And with the full revelation of God's grace in Jesus Christ there came a new dynamic and a pouring out of God's Spirit greater than ever before. The new covenant is characterised therefore by a new and more powerful manifestation of the Holy Spirit, though the substance of the covenant remains the same.

The *fourth* difference between the old and new covenants follows directly as a result of the third, viz. that the purpose of the greater manifestation of the Spirit in the Christian era is in order to enable God's people to preach the gospel with boldness and thus extend the covenant beyond the boundaries of the nation of Israel into the whole world.

Before Christ Israel was the only covenant nation. Of course individuals from the Gentile nations could and did become converts to Judaism, and it was the responsibility of the Jews to proclaim and bear witness to the message of salvation with which they had been entrusted (Rom. 2:19-20, 3:2), for God had chosen and appointed Israel to be a light to the Gentile nations (Is. 42:6). But Israel was the only *nation* in covenant with God. Since Christ, however, this has changed. The covenant is now for all nations. The Great Commission which Christ gave to His disciples confirms this. Christ has commanded us to "go therefore and make disciples of all *nations,* baptising them in the name of the Father, Son and Holy Spirit" (Matt. 28:19). The English translation of this verse does not really convey the true meaning however. We tend to read a sentence like this as if it said "go therefore and make disciples *from* all nations." This is because English does not have a verb meaning *to make a disciple of.*[4] The Greek does, however, and the phrase "all nations" is the direct object of this verb. In other words, Christ is here commissioning His followers to make disciples of the nations themselves, not simply disciples from among the nations. The covenant is therefore no longer restricted to Israel; it is for all the nations *as* nations.

Again the substance of the covenant remains the same, but in the Christian era the scope and application of the covenant is new. All nations are now to be claimed for Christ and disciplined under His rule and authority. The kingdoms of this world are to become the kingdom of our Lord and His Christ (Rev. 11:15).

Thus, to summarise: the covenant is a binding contract or treaty between God and mankind which defines man's relationship to God and to the rest of creation, with the following

---

4. *The Oxford English Dictionary* records the archaic verb *to disciple,* but its occurrence is rare. The nearest current English verb is *to discipline,* a term which, though it may have a nuance not normally associated with being a disciple of Christ in our day, is certainly not without merit in conveying the true nature of Christian discipleship.

qualification, that for man the covenant exists by virtue of his creation in the image of God, i.e. it is a fact of his creaturehood, not an agreement that he enters into as an autonomous consenting party. This covenant binds all men, and through man the whole creation. Man has broken the covenant by his sin, but this does not alter the covenantal nature of life and thus he must still face the consequences of his broken relationship with God. After the fall God redeemed His people by His free grace and thereby re-established or renewed His covenant with them. This renewed covenant relationship is entered into by faith, resulting in repentance—i.e a turning away from sin—and obedience to God's will as set down in the covenant law. The new covenant is the renewal in Jesus Christ of the one covenant of redemptive grace that has prevailed since the fall and the promise of deliverance given to Adam in the Garden of Eden, but it is a new or better covenant in four significant respects: (1) in Christ we have the *full revelation of God's redemptive purpose,* (2) the *sacrificial law* has been fulfilled and perfected in Christ's death as an atonement for sin and is therefore *no longer to be observed,* (3) since Pentecost and the pouring out of the Spirit the *dynamic* is new and far greater than ever before, and thus (4) the *scope* of the covenant is now far broader than ever before, encompassing the whole world and every nation on earth.

It should also be said here that the newness of the Christian covenant does not affect the abiding validity of the *terms* of the covenant, namely the law, since it is only the *form* of the covenant that has been changed and not the *substance* of it. Christ has not set aside the law. In principle the sacrificial law has not been set aside, it has been consummated in Christ's work on the cross, and this is the reason that the sacrificial rituals of the Old Testament are no longer to be observed. The *substance* of the sacrificial law has been put into force permanently by Christ's death, and this has resulted in a change in the *form* of its observance—viz. we now look to Jesus Christ alone and His death on the cross as the propitiation for our sin and thus the means by which we are reconciled with God. In other words we now observe the sacrificial law in Christ alone. Thus, the cross, rather than abrogating the law, testifies to its abiding validity. Christ came and died for sin precisely because the law could not be set aside, and by so doing He established its inviolability. God's law is thus to be our guide for life today just as it was for the nation of Israel long ago.

4. *The goal of the covenant.* Why is all this so important? Is it really necessary to know all this in order to live the Christian life? The answer is *yes.* It is not necessary to know all this in order simply to become a Christian, but it is necessary in order to live consistently as a Christian.[5] What do I mean by this?

It has been said that it is possible to have a saved soul and a wasted life. Not only is this possible, it is, unfortunately, a fact of life for many Christians today. This is because salvation is seen today primarily in terms of a private personal experience, or at best an experience or way of life which is confined to the boundaries of the institutional church. But this is a seriously distorted view of the Christian faith as it is set forth in the Bible. It is a view that has rendered the Christian community utterly impotent and irrelevant in our society today, and it must therefore be challenged and rejected if we are to *live* consistently as Christians.

The Christian faith is a total way of life. It is a way of

---

5. A saving knowledge of Christ, though it does presuppose a knowledge of sin and therefore a basic understanding of the doctrine of the law, does not presuppose an advanced or detailed knowledge of Scripture. Saving faith is naïve. However, this fact must not be used as an excuse for negligence and laziness in understanding the Christian faith (Heb. 2:1-3). Those who preach what they insist on calling "the simple gospel"—in truth it is their simplistic version of the gospel—and who resolutely refuse to come to terms with the full content of Scripture and the demands it makes on the whole of man's life, cannot hide behind the naïve nature of saving faith. Progress to maturity in understanding, as an essential aspect of the process of sanctification, is necessary in those who are true believers, and the failure of this indicates a basic problem in the Christian life.

thinking and living which embraces every aspect of man's life and being. If we are to live out this faith in the totality of our lives we must understand what the Scriptures have to say about *how* we should live. This brings us back to the covenant. We cannot escape the covenant. Christianity *is* the covenant. The life of faith revolves around the covenant. Why?

The covenant is God's plan for victory. What is that victory? It is the redemption of this fallen world. This redemption has been accomplished definitively in Christ's death and resurrection. But this victory at Calvary must now be worked out *in history* in the lives of God's people. We are commanded to claim the world for Christ. The apostle Paul says: "For though we walk in the flesh, we do not walk according to the flesh, for the weapons of our warfare are not of the flesh, but divinely powerful for the destroying of fortresses. We are destroying speculations and every lofty thing raised up against the knowledge of God, and we are taking every thought captive to the obedience of Christ" (2 Cor. 10:3-5).

This is the mandate that God has given to His people. We are to subject the world to the rule of Christ. This is the goal, the purpose which the covenant holds before us. This covenant is a covenant of *grace*, that is to say a relationship established upon the redeeming work of Jesus Christ and entered into by faith alone; but it is also a covenant of *dominion* in Jesus Christ. In other words, we have been saved by grace through faith in order that we might subdue the earth for the glory of God. The victory has already been won. It remains now for God's people to work out this victory in history.

Thus, the covenant gives us a goal, a purpose for living, viz. dominion in Christ. But it also gives us a means of achieving that goal, namely the law. It is the law which guides and instructs us about *how* we should live, both as individuals and as a society. We are saved by the grace of God that we might live for Christ. The law shows us how we are to live for Christ and thus how we are to achieve the dominion to which we are called in Christ. By applying God's law to our lives and to our society we shall begin a process of reformation or reconstruction in our land.

This must start with ourselves, with our own lives and those for whom we are responsible before God. But it must go beyond the personal to embrace the social dimensions of life also, and thus eventually to embrace the whole of life and society throughout the whole world. We are commanded to go into *all the world* and preach the gospel to every creature (Mark 16:15). In this way the kingdom of God will grow and Christ's rule will be extended over the whole earth.

Conclusion

Christ's victory at Calvary is worked out in history as the nations are evangelised and brought under the discipline of Christ. This is the Great Commission to which the people of God have been called. But we cannot hope to fulfil this mission if we do not seek to understand and apply the scriptures of both Old and New Testaments because it is these scriptures that set forth the covenant under which God has determined to redeem the world. Without growth in our knowledge of and commitment to the teachings of the Scriptures we are at best saved souls with wasted lives.

I am now back where I began, with the scriptures of the Old Testament. The scriptures of the Old Testament are vital for the Christian life because they set forth the terms, or law, of the covenant under which we have been redeemed and now live. The New Testament presupposes the abiding validity of the doctrines of the Old Testament, and the new covenant in Jesus Christ can only be understood properly in terms of the perspective of these scriptures.

It is thus impossible to live consistently as Christians and fulfil our Great Commission to make disciples of all nations if we are not prepared to study and apply to our lives and societies the teachings of the Old Testament, and the law of the covenant which it sets forth for all nations.

Appendix B

WORSHIP AND DOMINION

We are taught in Scripture by our Lord that those who worship God "must worship in spirit and in truth" (John 4:23). It is fundamentally important, therefore, that we understand the true nature of the worship that God requires of us.

In Hebrew the two basic words for worship are *shachah,* which means "to prostrate oneself, to humble oneself," and *habad,* which means "to serve, to work for." *Shachah* is equivalent to the Greek word *proskuneo* translated as "worship" in John 4:23, and is a physical act of stooping or bowing down in humility. With reference to God it is, of course, entirely worthless unless it symbolises a humble and willing submission to God and to His will.

The term *habad* has a far wider scope in that it includes the whole of man's life and actions. It signifies the service that God requires of man. Significantly, the substantive, *habodah,* also means "furniture." This may seem odd, but the logic of this is quite simple and instructive. Furniture serves a purpose, and that purpose is determined by the one who creates it. It is created entirely for the use and service of man. Furniture exists merely to serve man and his needs and therefore it does not have a purpose outside of the will and control of the one who owns it or uses it. In just the same way man was created to serve God according to His will. Man's life is embraced totally by God's sovereign will. No man has a legitimate purpose outside of God's design, and to turn ones' back on God and seek a life of autonomy is to make oneself a purposeless being without true meaning in life. It is to become the refuse of creation, and it is fitting that the eternal abode of those who seek such a life of autonomy is described in the New Testament as *Gehenna*, since Gehenna was a rubbish tip just outside Jerusalem where all kinds of refuse, including dead criminals and broken idols, was burned—the word *Gehenna* is translated as "hell" in the Authorised Version. Man's legitimate purpose is entirely taken up with God's will, and in the fulfilment of that purpose man serves, or labours, or worships by his service and labour, the God who created him. Thus, to deny God and His purpose for man is to make oneself the inhabitant of Gehenna.

The nature of the worship that God demands of man is in the New Testament further spelt out by the apostle Paul when he writes: "I beseech you therefore, brethren, by the mercies of God, that ye present your bodies a living sacrifice, holy, acceptable unto God, *which is your reasonable service*" [some translations read "spiritual worship"] (Rom. 12:1). The word translated "service" here is *latreia*, which means, first, "service," and then "divine service" or "worship." It is this word that is used to translate the word *habodah* in the Septuagint translation of the Old Testament. Thus, the apostle establishes the basic nature of worship by drawing attention to the fact that true worship is an intelligent, rational service to God by the whole man. This has significant implications.

First, the basic character of worship is *service* not experience. Neither *shachah* nor *habad*, nor their equivalents in the New Testament, refer to an experience or to a subjective emotional state of mind. Both refer to man's submission of himself to God, the former in the act of bowing down to God in adoration and humility as an expression of deference and submission to His lordship and sovereignty, the latter in a life of service and obedience to God. Worship is service, not experience.

Second, worship embraces the whole of life. We are to render our *bodies*—that is to say our whole being, not just the mind or the spirit—a holy sacrifice to God in all things. The body is engaged in the totality of life. Thus, with everything we are and in everything we do and think we are to serve God according to His will. In whatever field of study we are engaged, whatever vocation we have, whatever we do in our leisure time, we are to serve God according to His will, and only as we do this are we rendering to God the true worship that He demands of us.

By reducing the meaning of worship to what happens in church on Sunday, Christians have made the Christian religion irrelevant to life and consequently the church has become irrelevant as a cultural force in society. A concept of the faith that is essentially monastic has thus prevailed. Similarly, pietists see worship merely as something done by the inner man, whereas in the Bible worship is something done by the whole man in the whole course of his life. It embraces the totality of his life and being, in thought and in deed.

Thus, *third*, church worship, or Sunday service, is only one aspect of the worship that God requires from His people, though an essential and vitally important one. In church the people of God engage in corporate praise, prayer, thanksgiving, and receive teaching and instruction from the word of God. Also the sacraments of baptism and the Lord's supper are received. All these are important elements in the Christian life, but they do not constitute the whole of the worship that God requires of us, and when they exist merely by themselves, as a show done for effect once a week, we have a clear indication in Scripture that God finds such lip service unacceptable, What we do in Sunday service, therefore, is real and valid *only* in the greater context of a *life* of worship, i.e. of service to God.

Fourth, we are told that the worship God requires of us must be a *reasonable* service. The word here translated as "reasonable" (*logikos*) comes from the same word group from which we get the English words *logic* and *logical*. This especially needs to be borne in mind today when the nature of worship is seen almost entirely as emotional in character and devoid of rational content. Such worship is not acceptable to God. We are commanded to love the Lord our God with all our heart, with all our soul and with all our *mind* (Matt. 22:37), in other words with the totality of our being. The whole nature and course of our lives, including corporate worship on Sundays, must be a rational service to God. Thus, to attempt to worship God in an unknown language, whether it be through participation in the Tridentine Mass or "speaking in tongues," is a contradiction of the first and great commandment as expounded by our Lord.

This does not mean that we should idolise the intellect. But neither are we to neglect it. Our intellect is God-given and we are to use it to the best of our abilities, with all our might, in the service of God, just as we are to submit our emotional life to His service. Neither idolatry nor neglect is the correct approach to our minds as Christians. Christianity is not a heart religion; neither is it a head religion. It is a whole man religion which demands the total use of man's life and being in the service of God. Thus, to render a worship, whether in our daily lives or in corporate church services, that is not rational is to offer to God less than He demands of us.

Fifth, the exercise of dominion in Christ, since it is essential to the fulfilment of man's creation mandate and thus God's purpose in creating man, is an act of worship. We are called to dedicate our lives and vocations to God's service in accordance with His revealed purpose for His creation. This is man's creation or cultural mandate, given first in Genesis 1:28 and renewed and restated by our Lord Jesus Christ in Matthew 28:19-20. This mandate is the command to exercise dominion in the name of the Lord and thereby bring *all* things, every thought and practice of man, and every aspect of the world he has been given to rule over, into subjection to Jesus Christ. The exercise of dominion in Christ is thus an essential element of the service that God requires of man. To fail to pursue this dominion in Christ is to fail to render to God the worship He requires of man by a life of total service to God in His revealed will for the creation. It is to fail to glorify God in the way that He demands, and it is to render an inferior worship to the one who demands and rightfully claims our whole lives in His service.

The exercise of dominion in Christ is therefore an important part of the worship that God demands of His people. Thus, in Psalm 149 worship and dominion are inextricably linked together:

> Let the saints be joyful in glory: let them sing aloud upon their beds. Let the high praises of God be in their mouth, and a twoedged sword in their hand; to execute vengeance upon the heathen, and punishment upon the people; to bind their kings with chains, and their nobles with fetters of iron; to execute upon them the judgement written: this honour have all the saints. Praise ye the Lord. (vv. 5-9)

According to the translators of the Geneva Bible (1560) this Psalm is "An exhortation to the Church to praise the Lord for his victory and conquest that he giveth his saints against all man's power." Referring to v. 7 we are told that "This is chiefly accomplished in the kingdom of Christ, when God's people for just causes execute God's judgement against his enemies." The Puritans spoke of course from within the context of a Christian civilisation. They understood that the victory of the Christian church must lead to a Christian civilisation and the establishing of God's justice throughout the earth.

This is the future for which the Christian works in serving his Lord here on earth. The gospel must be preached throughout the whole world. The victory is certain, for God has given the nations to His Son as His inheritance (Ps. 2:8-12), and of the increase of His government and of peace there shall be no end (Is. 9:7). As God's people we have a glorious part in God's plan for the creation, and we look forward to the victory which is His, and through Christ ours also, both here on earth and in the resurrection. Our participation in God's purpose for His creation, and thus in His victory and conquest over sin and evil, is the service that God requires of us, and it is the totality of that service which constitutes the true worship that God demands of His people.

Sixth, this has far reaching implications for education. We are taught in the Scriptures that our children are to be brought up in the discipline and instruction of the Lord (Eph. 6:4). Few Christians would doubt that this involves teaching our children to worship God according to His word. Our children must understand the nature of the worship that God requires of man if they are to grow in grace and faith. But many fail to realise that the worship demanded by God from His people is far more than corporate praise in the congregation on Sundays and the pursuit of a private devotional life. To worship God means to *labour* or to *work* for God and His purpose in the whole course of one's life. Unless we seek to serve God, to work for God, in all that we do by pursuing the dominion that He requires of His people we shall fail to worship God according to His word.

Furthermore, if we fail to educate our children for dominion we shall fail to educate them for worship in the fullest sense, and thus hinder them from coming to God in Christ (Luke 18:16). The whole of man's life is to be a worship service to God, and therefore children must be educated to work for God, to labour "as to the Lord," in *all* things (Eph. 6:5-7). This necessitates an education based on godly learning and discipline in *all* things, all aspects of life, all academic disciplines etc.

A truly Christian education, therefore, is far broader than the traditional idea of "religious education" taught in most schools in our land. It is not a single subject dealing with a particular aspect of life, but embraces the whole of life, for in the whole course of our lives and in every thing we do we are to serve or work for God, and thereby fulfil the purpose for which He created and redeemed us in Jesus Christ. Only as we thus labour for God in all things shall we worship God according to His word, and therefore only as we educate our children accordingly shall we prepare them for a life of service and worship.

The worship that God demands of His people requires the provision of a godly education for our children, i.e. an education based on godly discipline and godly *learning* in all academic disciplines. The dominion to which we are called as God's people, and therefore the worship that we are to offer to our Redeemer, necessitates this process of godly learning and discipline, and to deny it to our children is to refuse to worship God according to His word, to hinder them from so doing also, and thus apostasy from the faith.

BIBLIOGRAPHY

J. E. Adams, *Back to the Blackboard* (Phillipsburg, New Jersey: Presbyterian and Reformed Publishing Company, 1982).

David Chilton, *Productive Christians in an Age of Guilt Manipulators* (Tyler, Texas: Institute for Christian Economics, [1981] 1985).

P. T. Bauer, *Indian Economic Policy and Development* (London: George Allen and Unwin Ltd., 1961).

P. T. Bauer, *Equality, the Third World and Economic Delusion* (London: Methuen, 1981).

William Boyd, *The History of Western Education* (London: Adam and Charles Black, [1921] 1966).

John Dewey, *Democracy and Education* (New York: The Free Press, [1916] 1944).

H. Dooyeweerd, *A New Critique of Theoretical Thought* (Presbyterian and Reformed Publishing Company, 1969), 2 vols.

H. Dooyeweerd, *In the Twilight of Western Thought* (Nutley, New Jersey: The Craig Press, 1980).

H. Dooyeweerd, *The Secularization of Science* (Memphis, TN: Christian Studies Centre).

Peter Gordon and John White, *Philosophers as Educational Reformers* (London: Routledge and Kegan Paul, 1979).

E. R. Green (ed.), *Jerusalem and Athens* (Phillipsburg, New Jersey: Presbyterian and Reformed Publishing Company, [1971] 1980).

Julian Henriques and William Anderson, "The Green man: The Re-emergence of a vital spirit—Father Earth" in *World Magazine*, no. 43 (November, 1990).

H. Hoeksema, *Reformed Dogmatics* (Grand Rapids, Michigan: Reformed Free Publishing Association, 1966).

S. L. Jaki, *Science and Creation: From eternal cycles to an oscillating universe* (Edinburgh: Scottish Academic Press, 1986).

Evan John Jones and Doreen Valiente, *Witchcraft, A Tradition Renewed* (London: Robert Hall, 1990).

A. R. S. Kennedy, "Education" in James Hastings (ed.), *A Dictionary of the Bible* (Edinburgh: T. & T. Clark, 1904), vol. I, pp. 646-652.

Nathan Morris, *The Jewish School: An Introduction to the History of Jewish Education* (London: Eyre and Spottiswoode, 1937).

G. North (ed.), *The Foundations of Christian Scholarship* (Vallecito, California: Ross House Books, 1976).

G. North, *Unholy Spirits: Occultism and New Age Humanism* (Ft. Worth, Texas: Dominion Press, 1986).

Michael Polanyi, *Personal Knowledge* (London: Routledge and Kegan Paul,[1958] 1962).

Karl R. Popper, *Conjectures and Refutations* (London: Routledge and Kegan Paul, [1963] 1972).

R. J. Rushdoony, *Intellectual Schizophrenia* (Phillipsburg, New Jersey: Presbyterian and Reformed Publishing Company, [1961] 1980).

R. J. Rushdoony, *The Messianic Character of American Education* (Phillipsburg, New Jersey: Presbyterian and Reformed Publishing Company, 1963).

R. J. Rushdoony, *The One and the Many* (Fairfax, Virginia: Thoburn Press, [1971] 1978).

R. J. Rushdoony,*The Institutes of Biblical Law* (Presbyterian and Reformed Publishing Company, 1973).

R. J. Rushdoony, *Revolt Against Maturity* (Vallecito, California: Ross House Books, 1977).

R. J. Rushdoony, *Salvation and Godly Rule* (Vallecito, California: Ross House Books, 1983).

R. J. Rushdoony, "Calvinism and Culture" in *Calvinism Today*, vol. I, no. 1 (January, 1991).

Cornelius Van Til, *A Survey of Christian Epistemology* (Phillipsburg, New Jersey: Presbyterian and Reformed Publishing Company).

Cornelius Van Til, *A Christian Theory of Knowledge* (Nutley, New Jersey: Presbyterian and Reformed Publishing Company, 1969).

Cornelius Van Til, *The Defense of the Faith* (Philadelphia, Pennsylvania: Presbyterian and Reformed Publishing Company, [1955] 1967).

Geerhardus Vos, *Biblical Theology* (Edinburgh: The Banner of Truth Trust, [1948] 1975).

Max Weber, *The Protestant Ethic and the Spirit of Capitalism* (London: Unwin Paperbacks, [1930] 1985).

E. G. West, *Education and the Industrial Revolution* (London and Sydney: B. T. Batsford Ltd., 1975).

Frances A. Yates, *Giordano Bruno and the Hermetic Tradition* (University of Chigago Press, 1964).

Frances A. Yates, *The Occult Philosophy in the Elizabethan Age* (London: Ark Paperbacks, [1979] 1983).

Further Reading

Louis Berkof and Cornelius Van Til (edited by Dennis E. Johnson), *Foundations of Christian Education* (Phillipsburg, New Jersey: Presbyterian and Reformed Publishing Company, 1990).

Samuel L. Blumenfeld, *How to Tutor* (Boise, Idaho: The Paradigm Company).

Samuel L. Blumenfeld, *NEA: The Trojan Horse in American Education* (Boise, Idaho: The Paradigm Company, 1984).

Samuel L. Blumenfeld, *The New Illiterates and How To Keep Your Child From Becoming One* (Boise, Idaho: The Paradigm Company, [1973] 1988).

David B. Cummings (ed.), *The Purpose of a Christian School* (Phillipsburg, New Jersey: Presbyterian and Reformed Publishing Company, 1979).

David B. Cummings (ed.), *The Basis for a Christian School* (Phillipsburg, New Jersey: Presbyterian and Reformed Publishing Company, 1982).

Jack Mechielsen (ed.), *No Icing on the Cake: Christian Foundations for Education* (Melbourne: Brooks-Hall Publishing Foundation, 1980).

G. North (ed.), *The Journal of Christian Reconstruction* vol. IV, no. 1 (Summer, 1977), *Symposium on Education* (Chalcedon Foundation, P. O. Box 158, Vallecito, California 95251).

R. J. Rushdoony, *By What Standard? An Analysis of the Philosophy of Cornelius Van Til* (Tyler, Texas: Thoburn Press, [1958] 1983).

R. J. Rushdoony, *The Philosophy of the Christian Curriculum* (Vallecito, California: Ross House Books, 1981).

Robert L. Thoburn, *The Children Trap: Biblical Principles for Education* (Ft. Worth, Texas: Dominion Press, 1986).

Cornelius Van Til, *Essays on Christian Education* (Nutley, New Jersey: Prebyterian and Reformed Publishing Company, [1971] 1977).

GENERAL INDEX